BUILDING THE RIGHT-SIZED LAYOUT

DESIGNING AND OPERATING A SMALL SWITCHING LAYOUT

Thomas Klimoski

Kalmbach
Media

Acknowledgements

I extend my sincere appreciation to all those that provided me information and photos. Without their help this book would not be possible. I would like to extend special thanks to Keith Armes, Michael Armstrong, Joe Atkinson, Stefan Bartelski, Alex Bogaski, George Bogatiuk, Scott Chatfield, John Farrington, Tom & Jean Ann Fausser, Tim Garland, Tom Holley, Tom Johnson, Tony Koester, James McNab, Lance Mindheim, David Payne, Seth Puffer, William Sampson, Jason Slaton, Greg Smith, Doug Tagsold, Jim Talbott, and Scott Thornton.

In addition, I would like to thank Eric White, the artists, and staff at Kalmbach Media for all their assistance with this book.

It is through the help and support of my family and friends, I have been able to enjoy this great hobby of model railroading. For that I am truly grateful and blessed.

Thomas Klimoski
Hiawassee, Ga.

ON THE COVER:
The Georgia Northeastern Railroad's Marble Hill Turn arrives to switch the two industries in Marble Hill, Georgia on Thomas Klimoski's layout. On the back cover, Long trains and sweeping scenery dominate Mike Armstrong's Rock Island Railroad layout, *Mike Armstrong;* **Tom Klimoski at his drafting table working on a track plan.**

Kalmbach Media
21027 Crossroads Circle
Waukesha, Wisconsin 53186
www.KalmbachHobbyStore.com

Published in 2021
26 25 24 23 22   2 3 4 5 6

Manufactured in China

ISBN: 978-162700-837-2
EISBN: 978-162700-838-9

Editor: Eric White
Book Design: Kelly Katlaps

Library of Congress Control Number: 2020940427

Contents

Introduction

What is the right-sized layout?

A right-sized layout is one that meets the modeler's operational needs while fitting into the space allocated for a model railroad. What is right-sized for one person may be a completely wrong choice for another. A right-sized layout can be any size, but more frequently building a smaller right-sized layout has been the best choice for many model railroaders. The goal of this book is to demonstrate that you may require less space than you thought to build a right-sized layout.

Layout size

It is difficult to place layouts into a specific size category, like small, medium, or large. A small layout may occupy a portion of a large space, yet another fills an entire small room. Aisle space and numerous other factors also impact a layout's size. Only using the square footage of a room that a layout occupies really is not a good indicator as to the layout's relative size. For the purposes of this book we'll consider a small layout one that could reasonably fit in a spare bedroom, or a portion of a larger room, but still leave space for other activities in the room.

Finding space

The question is how much space do you really need? Smaller layouts are gaining in popularity for numerous reasons. Modelers new to the hobby are learning the skills they need by building a small layout. That gives them the confidence they'll need if they attempt a larger layout in the future. Other modelers have found a small layout fits into their busy lives and still gives them the operations they desire. Veteran modelers who have downsized their homes have discovered the benefits of working on a smaller layout that still allows them to enjoy the hobby while not taking up much space in their new home.

The case for smaller layouts

Many times smaller layouts are thought of as being less fulfilling than a larger layout. This type of thinking is discouraging to those who may only have limited space in which to build a layout. They figure unless they have a large space for a layout, why bother building one? Fortunately, lots of modelers have disregarded this type of thinking and found that a small switching layout is perfect for them and fits their needs.

A small layout can easily be incorporated into a larger space while still allowing use of the remainder of the room for other activities. Spare bedrooms are also the perfect candidate to build a small layout. Depending on how the benchwork is constructed, the room can still be used

By using Ikea shelving, a lighting valance, and providing a nicely finished museum-type display for his switching layout, Alex Bogaski has found a space for his layout along one wall in his living room. This design demonstrates that a model train layout can complement the room décor and offer hours of enjoyable operations. *Alex Bogaski*

for multiple other functions, including a workbench for assembling models and storage of modeling supplies.

How much time do you want to allocate to building a layout? Many times modelers don't anticipate the amount of time it takes to build a model railroad. When building a smaller layout, each phase of construction is completed in a reasonable time period. Seeing progress motivates you to continue and not get discouraged or overwhelmed with one task of building a layout.

There are many things that a modeler can do that will make a small layout operate like a much larger one. A layout does not have to be large to have an enjoyable operating session. To add realism and slow down an operating session, crews can replicate many prototype procedures and safety practices. These procedures can be applied to help a layout operating session last longer while not adding any additional track or industries.

Enjoying the hobby

Model railroading is a hobby that involves multiple skills and different ways to enjoy it. From track planning, carpentry, electrical work, scenery, and weathering, to realistic operating sessions there are so many ways to participate. As you build a layout, your skills will improve, so practice enhancing your modeling skills with building a small layout now so if and when you decide to build your "dream layout," you'll be ready. Until that day arrives, build a right-sized layout and have fun. You may just find that a right-sized layout *is* your dream layout.

1

The right-sized layout

The biggest decisions model railroaders face when they choose to build a layout is determining its operational design and size. What is the "right-sized" layout for you is a very personal choice. Each model railroader has his or her own goals and objectives, which has an impact on layout design and the space it will require.

2

Determining the right-sized layout for you

John Farrington's Railserve layout, above, based on a prototype in Pennsylvania, fits nicely in a spare room in his apartment. The layout is L-shaped with the longest leg being 11 feet along one wall, and a new 5-foot extension added to one end. The layout has provided an opportunity for John to try new modeling techniques and improve his already exceptional modeling skills. *John Farrington*

Long trains and sweeping scenery dominate Mike Armstrong's Rock Island Railroad layout. The layout represents the upper Midwest from St. Paul, Minn., to Kansas City, Kan., in the 1960s. The track plan is prototypical with large areas of beautiful rural scenery. With his large radius super-elevated curves, Mike can easily run 30 car trains on his layout. *Mike Armstrong*

Operational goals

One of the first questions to ask yourself is what type of operations do you enjoy? Do you like switching operations, mainline running, or a combination of both? This decision will have a large influence on the operational design and size of your layout. Switching operations can easily be accommodated on a smaller layout, **1**, while mainline running will normally require a much larger layout, **2**. Once you have determined the type of operations you want, then you can consider the space you have available to build your layout

If you are not sure which type of operations you prefer, then reflect on how you like to observe the prototype. Do you enjoy sitting trackside and viewing trains roll by, or do you prefer watching a local going about its switching duties? There is not a right or wrong answer, but the decision you make will affect the type of layout you should build.

If you enjoy mainline running and watching trains' progress around the layout with limited or no stops, then you will need to design a larger layout with greater distance between the towns or key scenes. Trains moving at a realistic track speed cover a great distance in a short period of time on a model railroad. To compensate for the distance needed, these types of layouts can be designed to have shallower shelf-type mainline scenes between deeper town areas to reduce the amount of space required, **3**.

For those who want to model a switching operation, that can be accommodated in a smaller layout. Switching operations are performed at a slower speed, which allows for a smaller layout to realistically replicate the time it takes the prototype to complete the operations. The subject for a switching layout can be an industrial area, a port-to-rail interchange, small town, or a yard.

Tom Fausser models the South Brooklyn Terminal in 1954 to 1959. His layout features an urban environment with sharp curves and a car float operation using 44- and 70-ton locomotives, **4**. The smaller locomotives easily negotiate the tight curves and look appropriate on the layout.

Modelers Dale Baker and Jason Slaton model port-to-rail operations on their bedroom-sized layouts. Dale models the Port of Catoosa, near Tulsa, Okla., while Jason models the Port of Fernandina, in Fernandina Beach, Fla., **5**. Numerous industries are located around both facilities and offer lots of operations in a relatively compact area. These facilities typically use small switching locomotives operated by a short line or industrial railroad, **6**.

Another option is to include both switching and mainline running.

3 In this image of Mike Armstrong's Rock Island layout, five Rock Island GP35 locomotives pass over Battle Creek Bridge near Dayton's Bluff, Minn. The scene is built on a 10"-wide shelf to allow better visibility for the lower level of this double-deck layout and provide for longer runs between the towns. The minimal depth is offset by an effective backdrop and realistic scenery along the line.

4 In these images from Tom Fausser's South Brooklyn Terminal layout, he accurately captures the look of an urban and heavy industrial area with sharp curves and large structures. The layout is set in the 1954 to 1959 time period, and uses 44- and 70-ton locomotives. The layout also includes a car float operation. These types of urban areas make an excellent subject for a model railroad. *Jean Ann Fausser*

This track plan, designed by Lance Mindheim (www.shelflayouts.com) for Jason Slaton, is based on the prototype Fernandina Beach, Fla., port area served by the First Coast Railroad. The layout includes several prototype industries as well as a port area where cargo is off-loaded from ships. In this scene from Jason's layout, a locomotive switches cars in the small yard. *Track plan by Lance Mindheim, used with permission*

5

One way to accomplish this goal in a limited space is to model one town on a railroad main line, **7**. This design allows for main line trains to pass through the scene and be enjoyed as a railfan would, but still have the local stop in town to do some switching. These layouts require a sizable staging yard to hold the trains off stage until they are scheduled to appear. With careful planning, a layout operation centered on one town can be adapted to fit in a smaller space.

Crew size

The next factor to consider is how many operators you want or need to operate your layout. Are you planning to operate the layout yourself, or do you want to have operators over for an "ops" session? Knowing how many operators you plan to have needs to be considered as you design your layout, **8**.

Aisle space is overlooked many times when designing a layout. Operators need to be able to work and operate the layout without feeling crowded. A good rule of thumb from the party planning industry is that each person needs about 5 to 6 square feet of space to feel comfortable in a standing environment. Determine the number of operators required and assure you have adequate aisle space based on the above guideline for a comfortable, uncrowded experience, **9**.

If you build it will they come? Before you build your layout you should survey other model railroaders in your area to see if anyone is interested in operating on your proposed layout. Why build a large layout if you can't get

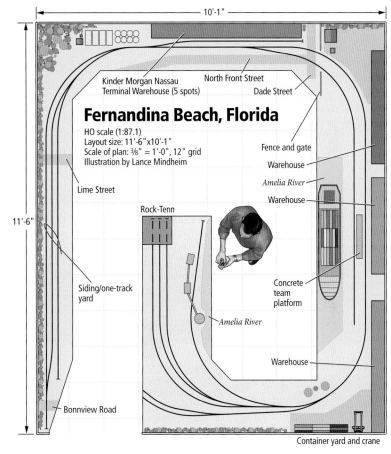

Fernandina Beach, Florida

HO scale (1:87.1)
Layout size: 11'-6" x 10'-1"
Scale of plan: 3/8" = 1'-0", 12" grid
Illustration by Lance Mindheim

Kinder Morgan Nassau Terminal Warehouse (5 spots)
North Front Street
Dade Street
Fence and gate
Warehouse
Amelia River
Warehouse
Lime Street
Rock-Tenn
Concrete team platform
Siding/one-track yard
Amelia River
Warehouse
Bonnview Road
Container yard and crane

a crew to come over to operate? Joining your local National Model Railroad Association division, a model railroad operating group, or club could give you a good indication of the number of people interested in operations and a list of potential operators.

Time

After considering your operational goals and crew size, the next factor to consider is time. Time can be broken down into two categories, length of

operating sessions and the time to perform operating tasks.

How long do you want an operating session to last? Surveys indicate most found a 3-hour operating session was about right. Many small layout owners prefer shorter ops sessions of around an hour. These sessions can be very informal with the layout owner operating alone switching a few cars or running a few trains around the layout.

James McNabb designed his previous Iowa Interstate Railroad

First Coast Railroad locomotive no. 1605, owned by Genesee and Wyoming Inc., was originally built in 1950 as a GP7 for the Atlantic Coast Line Railroad. The unit was rebuilt as a GP16 and still earns its keep switching the Fernandina Beach, Fla., port line. Four-axle locomotives and short lines are a perfect fit for a small switching layout. *Keith Armes*

6

7

In *Model Railroad Planning 2020*, Trains.com executive producer David Popp designed an HO scale track plan of his hometown of Crystal Lake, Ill. The plan features a large staging area on a traverser that allows for numerous trains to be staged and operated during an ops session. A local switcher also serves the numerous industries on the layout. This layout very nicely blends the operational requirements for through trains, passenger trains and local switching in a relatively small space.

Crystal Lake 1950

HO scale (1:87.1)
Layout size: 10 x 15 feet
Scale of plan: ⅜" = 1'-0", 12" grid
All turnouts no. 5 unless noted
Illustration by Rick Johnson

⊕ Find more plans online in the Trains.com Track Plan Database.

Open
Bowman Dairy
Backdrop
Water column
3"
0"
¾"
Crystal Lake Avenue
Open
Houses
Office
3"
Water column
Farm implements dealer
Feed warehouse
Coal bin
70-foot turntable
Coaling tower
C&NW Geneva Division line to Elgin, Ill.
Steel water tank
Rosenthal Lumber Co.
0"
½"
Brick platform with partial canopy
To Chicago
Parking lot
Depot
Grant Avenue
Water column
Freight house
Elevated crossing gate shack
Crystal Lake Lumber
Building cut-away to reveal interior
Open dock
Workbench space under traverser
7-foot traversing table six staging tracks
McHenry County Farmers Coop Association
To Janesville and Madison, Wis.
Standard Oil Co.
F. Schraam greenhouses
Cemetery
No. 6½ curved
No. 6½ curved
3"
2¾"
Walkup Avenue
Coal bin
Ice track
30" swing-up section
Storage shed
2½"
No. 7½ curved
No. 8 curved
Entryway

(IAIS) Grimes Line to focus on the operations of the local as it worked the industries along the line. A typical operating session on his layout took about one hour to complete, **10**.

With a small layout it is possible to set up several jobs that operate in sequence. That way an ops session can last as long as the operators want it to. Planning for operations should be considered when designing the layout. Think about how each train or local would be operated, and approximately how long each job would take.

One of the concerns with building a small layout is that it won't provide enough operations to keep things interesting, and have a decent-length ops session. On my Georgia Northeastern Railroad layout, I have a North Local switch job that includes seven industry locations and one off-spot siding in a town on my layout, **11**. The industrial area switched is approximately one third of my entire layout. This portion of the layout is an L shape, with the long leg being 10'-6" long, and 9'-2" on the shorter leg. A staging cassette is connected to the end of the longest leg. The local departs staging and switches the industries before returning to the staging yard. Not all industries are switched each ops session. The typical number of cars set out and picked up is six to eight. Operating at normal switching speeds, it takes approximately 1 hour to complete the local job. This one switch job is more than adequate for many of my guest operators.

To break it down even further, let's look at how much time it takes to perform specific switching tasks within the ops session. I performed these time studies on my layout following prototype procedures of

Two-person crews work the trains on Joe Atkinson's Iowa Interstate Railroad Subdivision 4 West End layout. Joe accounted for the crew size needed to operate his layout during the design phase and allowed adequate aisle space for members to follow their trains around the layout. *Joe Atkinson*

Clean, uncluttered, and spacious aisles are a signature feature of Mike Armstrong's Rock Island Railroad layout. In addition to generous aisle space, Mike's train room includes plenty of natural and fluorescent light. All of this provides a comfortable environment for his guests to operate his layout.

Iowa Interstate (IAIS) locomotive no. 708, a GP38-2, with its local consist rounds a curve on James McNab's IAIS Grimes Industrial Track Line. The layout featured switching in a couple of towns along the line. The relaxed pace of a local was exactly what James wanted to replicate on his layout. **He found the perfect prototype with the IAIS Grimes Industrial Track Line.** *James McNab*

The Georgia Northeastern North Local arrives in Marietta, Ga., on Tom's layout to switch the industries there. Switching the various industries can take over an hour to perform as crews plan their moves to operate efficiently. No complicated switching moves are required, just a relaxed pace of pulling and spotting cars. This one switch job is more than enough of an operating session for many visitors to the layout.

stopping between movements and to align turnouts. The time started when the crew makes the cut on the main line, and stopped when the crew had re-assembled its train. The speed during the switching was not excessively fast or slow, just a realistic pace of 5 to 10 mph for movements and slow gentle couplings, **12**.

After conducting the time studies, I came up with the following information:

• Setting out one car at an industry, 2 minutes 30 seconds;

• Picking up and setting out one car at an industry, 5 minutes;

• Moving one car to access a pickup, setting out an inbound car, then re-spotting the first car, 8 minutes.

Now with these time studies you can define how long an operating session will last on your layout. Determine the number of industries to be switched, the number of inbound and outbound cars, and how those car movements are made. Remember that picking up or setting out two cars coupled together takes the same amount of time as one car if the industry is not spot specific.

As an example, if you have four industries on your layout to switch with three of the industries being simple

pull-then-spot-a-car movements, and one industry where the crew needs to pull a car, then re-spot the car after pulling and spotting a car behind it, your total time for the switching movements is 23 minutes. Add approximately 20 to 30 minutes of "run time" for the movements between the industry locations and for making any runaround movements. This run time factor varies based on the design and size of your layout. Once you add both of these times together, the industry switching time and the run time, you have a basic time frame for an ops session. In the above example, switching four industries would take approximately 43 to 53 minutes. In later chapters I'll discuss options to

12

13

The work of the local has not changed much in the past 100 years. The only major difference is the crew size. It still takes about the same amount of time to pull and spot cars on the prototype today as it did years ago. Time studies of switching cars on a layout can help you determine the number of industries you want to include on your layout and the length of an operating session. Here the local spots a boxcar load of bricks at the team track.

William Sampson finished a guest bedroom in his basement, which also serves as his layout room. He installed drywall, flooring (currently covered to protect it), lighting, shelving, and a Murphy bed (on the right side of the photo) before beginning building his layout. The room now is a very comfortable environment and an excellent use of space for a layout. *William Sampson*

Water can be a huge issue with a layout in a basement as James McNab discovered. Plumbing issues required removal of his IAIS Grimes Industrial Line layout to repair the problems. Once the repairs were completed he installed an interlocking rubber floor mat and began construction on his new IAIS Hills Industrial Spur layout. Time spent resolving any water issues before building a layout will pay off in the long run by avoiding dealing with them later once the layout is built and access is much more difficult. *Two photos by James McNab*

14

add time to an ops session by following prototype procedures or adding operational details.

Layout room options

Now that we have looked at determining your operational goals, crew size, and time requirements for an operating session, let's take a look at finding room for your layout. In a perfect world we would all have a large unobstructed room in which to build our layouts. The reality is that many times we have to work with what we have, even if it is less than ideal. But don't worry, you can still "find" some space to have a layout, you just have to

look at different options that can work for you.

One of the first places that comes to mind when looking for a layout room is the basement. The problem is that basements can range from completely finished to something you would see in a horror movie. A layout room should be a comfortable, climate-controlled space with adequate lighting, **13**. If your basement is far from this requirement, time and money spent to bring it up to a finished space will pay off when it is a comfortable space you want to work in and operate a model railroad.

The other caution with installing a layout in a basement is the possibility

of water leaks. Several layout owners have experienced water issues in their basements that required removal of the layout to make the necessary repairs, **14**. The water issues can range from water leaking through the walls, to backed-up sump pumps, to plumbing issues. Steps taken to eliminate potential water problems before installation of a layout is highly recommended.

What if your house does not have a basement or it is already dedicated to other uses? The next place to look at for a layout space is a spare bedroom. Most standard-sized bedrooms are at least 10 x 10 feet, and many are larger

15

Jason Slaton's Port of Fernandina layout fits into a spare-bedroom-sized room in his basement. The layout can easily accommodate a two-person crew, one as engineer and the other as conductor, for switching operations on the layout. In addition, a second crew could work the small yard on the left while the first crew works the industries on the line.

16

George Bogatiuk's layout is built along one wall in his garage and allows him room to store his hockey gear below. The layout models the Missouri Pacific in southeast Missouri and northeast Arkansas in 1978. Operations are performed with a two-person crew, one working the yard and the other working the industrial area. Most trains are five cars and the layout provides plenty of operations for the crew. George included a seam between the yard and industrial area that will allow for future expansion as space allows. *George Bogatiuk*

17

Tom's previous CSX Hawksridge Subdivision layout was built in a two-car garage in Miami, Fla. The layout featured a removable peninsula that was hung on the wall when not being used to allow room for a car to be parked inside. In addition, removable sections were also installed across the garage door opening to expand the operations completely around the perimeter of the garage, allowing for a continuous run.

18

Bernard Kempinski's Port of Los Angeles layout shares space in the family room of his house. The layout is built on Ikea shelves and fits attractively within the casual living space of his home. Bernard stained the posts black to match the electronics and left the shelves natural wood. The layout is a compact prototype version of the Port of Los Angeles and operations involve a two-person crew working one train at a time. *Bernard Kempinski*

than that. The good part of building a layout in a bedroom is that the space is normally climate-controlled and finished. A bedroom-sized layout is the perfect size for a small switching layout and can comfortably provide operating sessions for two to four operators, **15**.

Another option for a bedroom layout is storing the layout under the bed and then sliding it out to operate. The layout could be built in two sections each 5 feet long and 18" wide. The two sections could then be placed on removable legs, or folding saw horses, and connected together to form a layout that is 10 feet long by 18" wide, perfect for a small switching layout. Structures would be removable and stored in a container when not on the layout.

Garages, while not ideal, can also be a location for a layout, **16**. An around-the-walls type layout will fit inside the garage while still leaving room to park a car inside if necessary, **17**. If it is possible to convert the garage into a finished room, it will make the layout space much more comfortable and reduce the dust and dirt that is normally found in garages.

The final option for a layout room is a mixed-use type room arrangement. A model railroad can peacefully coexist in a space that is used for other functions, **18**. If the layout is a shelf style placed in the corner of the room, it leaves the rest of the room available for other uses such as a family room or home office. The key with such a layout is to finish the layout similar to a diorama that is displayed at museum. The fascia should complement the room décor, and cluttered storage should be hidden or eliminated from under the layout. Shelving under

20 Highly detailed scenes, like this one on John Farrington's Railserve layout, are easier to accomplish and have a higher visibility on a smaller layout. The slower speed of the switching operations give crews time to appreciate the finer details and scenery on the layout. *John Farrington*

19 The addition of a lighting valance improves the finished look of Alex Bogaski's switching layout. The layout's prominent position in the living room of his home required a museum-like diorama presentation to fit with the décor of the room. *Alex Bogaski*

the layout can be used for books or displaying models. Adding a lighting valance helps to finish off the look and provides excellent light for the models, **19**. The layout can be viewed much as a piece of artwork would be at a gallery.

There are many solutions to finding space for a layout—you just have to look around. A small layout may be the perfect solution to incorporating a layout into the space you have.

Small layout advantages

While each size of layout has its own advantages, a small layout provides several benefits that appeal to modelers. The advantages include quicker construction, lower cost, easier maintenance, higher level of detail, and possible portability.

A small layout can be quickly constructed and the modeler can be up and running trains within a few weeks of starting construction. This faster pace of construction helps keep the modeler motivated and moving forward with projects rather than being bogged down with a project that seems to have no end. Each phase of construction is less overwhelming when it can be completed in a reasonable time period.

21 Alex Bogaski's layout features switching one spot-specific industry, Univar Industries, a food processing plant. The extra moves required to get the cars in the correct order for each spot adds time to the ops session. This compact layout offers hours of enjoyable switching operations. The layout can easily be moved when the time comes to relocate to a new house. *Alex Bogaski*

The expression "Money is no object" does not apply to most people's hobby budget. There is only so much money that can be spent on hobby-related items before it causes stress in a household relationship. Small layouts can be built without putting a large dent in the family budget. The cost of track, structures, and rolling stock are more manageable when building a smaller layout. After all, you don't need hundreds of cars and locomotives to operate on a small layout.

I have not found one model railroader yet who enjoys cleaning track. While it is not a project that anyone enjoys, it must be done so trains operate reliably. A small layout allows for quicker routine maintenance chores and more reliable operation because it is easier to maintain.

22 Long trains with multiple locomotives, like this scene from Mike Armstrong's Rock Island Railroad layout, are better accommodated on a larger layout. Mike enjoys seeing long trains wind their way through open country scenes, so building a large double-deck model railroad was the "right-sized" layout choice for him.

Fillmore Avenue Roundhouse

HO scale (1:87.1)
Layout size: 12'-0" x 30"
Scale of plan: ½" = 1'-0", 12" grid
Three 4-foot layout sections comprise a layout 12 feet long.
All turnouts no. 6 unless noted
Illustration by Rick Johnson

⊕ Find more plans online in the Trains.com Track Plan Database.

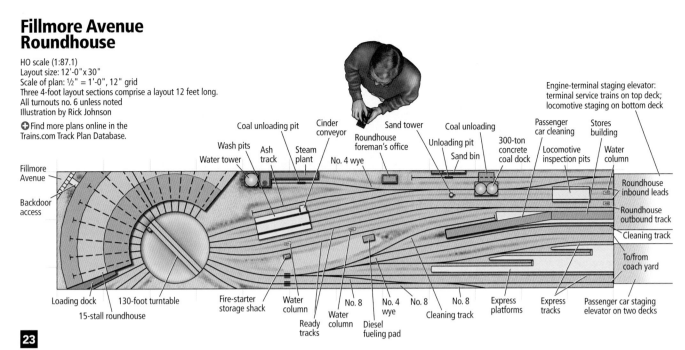

23

In *Model Railroad Planning 2015*, Rick De Candido designed a track plan centered on an engine terminal. A staging area on one end provides a connection to the "outside world" and the rest of the railroad. Operations revolve around the various activities that occur in an engine terminal. This type of layout allows for larger steam locomotives to be operated in a compact space.

24

Mike Armstrong designed a double deck layout to accomplish his goals of seeing trains travel across the open country served by the Rock Island Railroad. In many locations the upper deck is a shallow width to allow better viewing of the lower deck. Trains access the upper deck from a helix at two separate locations on the line. Building a double-deck layout effectively doubled the length of the main line run on Mike's layout. *Mike Armstrong*

25

Passenger train operations on a layout require long runs between stations to look realistic. After this stop in Des Moines, Iowa, this train still has about a third of the lower deck and all of the upper deck of Mike Armstrong's Rock Island to cross before it reaches staging. Even with compressed distances between the prototype stations modeled, running a passenger train from one end of the layout to the other can take over 20 minutes. *Mike Armstrong*

With a small layout it is possible to concentrate on details. As the trains often operate slower on a smaller layout, the crew has time to "take in the scenery." This includes structures as well as the rolling stock. Smaller layouts can more easily be superdetailed, which gives a layout a more finished look, **20**.

Small layouts can be built with portability in mind. When the day comes to move, the layout can be quickly packed up and moved without too much trouble. Modelers don't have to worry that all their hard work on layout will be wasted, **21**.

These advantages are just a few of the benefits of building small layout. Each modeler must decide if his or her operational goals, crew size, and layout room requirements will be met with a smaller layout. While a small layout may be the best choice for some model railroaders, there are times when only a larger layout will satisfy their operational goals.

Small layout challenges

For those modelers with specific needs and wants, a small layout may not be the right choice. If you want to run

Layouts that feature switching a yard, such as Joe Atkinson's IAIS Railroad Subdivision 4 West End layout, left, or switching industrial areas, like Tom's Georgia Northeastern Railroad's Marble Hill industries, are ideally suited to slow-speed operations. The slower speeds make the layout operate like a much larger one. *IAIS photo by Joe Atkinson*

26

large steam locomotives, replicate timetable and train order (TTTO) operations, run high-speed passenger or through freight trains, or multiple-unit locomotive lashups, then you will need a much larger layout to accomplish your goals, **22**.

Typically, curves on a small layout will be much below the recommended radius for large steam locomotives to operate reliably and look appropriate. By keeping a 24" minimum radius for HO scale, a small layout will accommodate most diesel locomotives, but larger radius curves should be planned where possible. If you want to run large steam locomotives, but only have room for a small layout, consider only modeling a locomotive service facility. This would give you the ability to operate large locomotives while avoiding the tight curves, **23**.

Timetable and train order operation requires great distances between towns for the train crew to accurately replicate following the prototype rules and regulations for such type of operation. It breaks the illusion if crews can look up the line to the next town to see if they are able to proceed rather than following their timetable and train orders. If you desire TTTO operations on your layout then you will need to build a larger layout, possibly a double deck, with long distances between towns. Double-deck layouts can add the distance necessary to replicate the longer runs desired for

27

Scratchbuilding structures, like this small shed from Jason Slaton's Port of Fernandina layout, is a great way to improve your modeling skills. Completing these smaller projects give the modeler confidence and the experience necessary to accomplish larger projects.

operations to be realistic, **24**. Small layouts do a better job of replicating micro-operations, the interaction of the railroad with the customer, rather than macro-operations, which represent a large railroad transportation system. If you want to replicate TTTO operations and only have a limited space you could use a fast clock and have the local crew follow the procedures of clearing the main line at certain times to represent the first-class trains passing through on the main.

High speed freights and passenger trains also require a great distance between towns or stations, **25**. Using a speed calculator for HO scale, a model train traveling at 29 scale mph will cover 10 feet of track in 20 seconds, or 6" per second. On a small layout with

limited track length, trains traveling 30 mph would quickly be out of room and off the layout into staging within a very short period of time. Smaller layouts are more suited to slow-speed operations and switching type duties, **26**.

What is the right choice?
Now that we have discussed the types of operational goals, crew size, time factors, and room options, what is the right choice for you? It all comes back to the "right-sized" layout for your specific situation. Small layouts can be as just as much fun to operate as the larger ones and give you a chance to showcase and improve your modeling skills, **27**. What are you waiting for? It's time to start planning that layout you have been envisioning for a long time.

1

CHAPTER TWO

Track planning

Now that you have decided to build your layout, the next step is to develop a track plan, **1**. The most difficult part of designing a track plan is starting off with a blank piece of paper or computer screen and determining what you want to design in the space you have. There are numerous books on the market that cover track planning and are a good place to start before you draw the first track line on your paper or computer screen. One book that is a must-read for anyone designing a track plan is *Track Planning for Realistic Operation* by John Armstrong. In this chapter I will highlight some of the key factors that need to be contemplated as you design your layout.

Factors to consider when designing your track plan

Track plans can be hand drawn or use a computer program. If choosing to hand draw the track plan, use graph paper and keep the drawing to scale. It is best to use templates for the turnouts to prevent unrealistic track angles for the diverging routes. It is much easier to erase lines on the paper than it is to pull up track that has already been laid, so spending time on this phase of layout planning and design results in a smooth-running model railroad.

2

Vast amounts of information can be obtained from observing the prototype. In this photo taken in Florida, note the differences in track maintenance and the ballast profile from the yard to the main line on the right. Also notice how all the switch stands are on the same side of the yard lead and away from the diverging yard tracks.

3

Track maintenance on this CSX branch line in Miami is certainly not to the same standards as a high-speed rail line. Many portions of the line are covered in tall weeds and grass. Maximum track speed on these types of branch lines are normally no more than 10 mph, which makes them excellent candidates for a small model railroad.

4

How you lay and ballast the track can make it look like different sizes of rail. All the track in the photo is Micro Engineering code 70. The siding track in the foreground is laid directly on the layout base, and ballast and weeds were allowed to cover the ties. The main line track was laid on cork roadbed and a standard ballast profile was used to replicate a more maintained track.

Look to the prototype

With a small layout, the track planning is more critical as every square inch is important to the overall design. While having limited space may seem to be a problem when you are track planning, it actually allows you to focus on what is most important to you and incorporate that into the design. One of the best places to get inspiration for your track plan is to take a look at the prototype.

It does not matter if your layout is freelanced or prototype-based, all modelers should look at prototype trackwork and design to help make their layouts as realistic as possible, **2**. If you are modeling a specific era and region, obtain photos of the location in the year you are modeling for reference. Photos will show how the right-of-way was maintained during the period you are modeling. Also look at the weight of rail found on the main line and sidings. Depending on the size and number of trains on the line, the rail weight will be heavier or lighter to accommodate the use. Branch lines and short lines will generally also have lighter weight rail and less maintained rights-of-way, **3**.

In HO scale, code 83 (.083" high) rail has become a standard size of track to represent mainline trackage. Code 70 and 55 (.070" and .055" respectively) can be used to represent lighter-weight rail found on sidings and secondary lines. Many modelers use one size of rail for the main lines and transition to a smaller size for sidings and yards. Transition rail joiners are used to connect the different sizes of rail together.

Another option is to place the mainline track on cork or Homasote roadbed and lay the same weight track for the sidings on thinner sheet cork or directly on the layout baseboard. When ballasting the track on the siding, allow some of the ballast to cover the ties and bring the weeds and scenery right up to the track. On the main line, maintain a standard ballast profile and

it will look larger than the track on the siding, giving the illusion of different weights of rail, **4**.

Once you have determined the general condition of the track, look at what industries the railroad serves. Does the railroad mainly serve a couple of major industries like coal or steel? Or does the railroad serve a wide variety of smaller customers? By looking at the prototype and using it for inspiration, your model railroad will look more realistic and believable, especially if it is freelanced.

The final prototype component to consider is, where do the railcars or trains originate and terminate? It may take a little work, but by doing research you can determine where most of the railroad's main yards or interchange points are. For our model railroads, it is important to have a way to connect our layouts to the rest of the rail network. This can be accomplished in several ways including hidden and visible staging as well as including an interchange yard replicating the rest of the rail system.

While compromises will always have to be made, you can now begin to set the theme for the layout and start narrowing down what you will be able to include on your layout after looking at the above elements. This is the point where choices will have to be made as what to include and what to leave out. It is always enticing to try to squeeze

The High Bridge on the prototype Iowa Interstate Railroad's Subdivision 4 West End is a signature scene recognized by all who live there or have visited the area. Joe Atkinson knew that if he wanted to realistically model the area he had to include it on his model railroad as a Layout Design Element (LDE). As soon as visitors to his layout see the bridge, they immediately recognize and relate to the area that Joe is modeling. *Joe Atkinson*

5

One of the most identifiable areas on the prototype Georgia Northeastern Railroad is the locomotive service facility in Tate, Ga. The sand tower is a prominent feature and was a key component to replicating the area as an LDE. On the model, the sand tower was scratchbuilt based on estimated measurements of the prototype. The fuel service area and storage tanks were placed in the same locations as they are at the prototype facility. The structure was kitbashed from Pikestuff kits. Though smaller than the prototype, it captures the general look and design of the building.

6

in one more industry or track, but resisting the temptation will help make the layout look better and operate more realistically.

Layout Design Elements (LDE)

Both freelance and prototype modelers benefit from duplicating key or signature scenes from the prototype. Tony Koester, editor of *Model Railroad Planning* and author of numerous books, has coined the term "Layout Design Element" (LDE) that describes modeling a specific scene as accurately as possible to capture the look and feel of a prototype scene or element. By replicating this prototype element, it automatically gives the

viewer a reference to understand what and where you are modeling. Tony states, "My entire railroad, based on the Nickel Plate Road's St. Louis line between Frankfort, Ind., and Charleston, Ill., is nothing more than a series of LDEs connected by segments of rural main line.

"A LDE can be an industry, station, town, or a key scenic element on the prototype railroad. These LDEs can be combined together to form a very realistic representation of a prototype railroad."

Look at the railroad you want to model, or take inspiration from, and determine the key LDEs you want to include on your layout. These

LDEs should instantly place your layout in the region and era you are modeling. Anyone who is familiar with the area should easily recognize the scene. Joe Atkinson, who models the Iowa Interstate Railroad, selected the High Bridge as one of his LDEs that immediately makes his layout recognizable to those familiar with the line, **5**. Freelancers can take LDEs from different prototype railroads in the same geographic area and connect them together to make a plausible freelanced railroad.

On the prototype Georgia Northeastern Railroad, the locomotive service facility in Tate, Ga., is a prominent location on the railroad. By

7

The staging yard on Tim Garland's Seaboard Central layout is placed in a room adjoining his layout room. The yard has storage for four trains and is his connection to the rest of the rail network. This arrangement gives his trains a place to come from or go to that is away from the main layout. *Tim Garland*

8

A swing up staging yard was part of the design for the Winston-Salem Southbound project railroad designed by David Popp. The staging yard measures 35" long and its two tracks can hold up to seven 40-foot cars. The staging yard greatly enhances the operations on this small layout. *William Zuback*

9

The staging cassette for Tom's layout is easily installed before an operating session. The cassette is 5'-6" long by 8" wide and has two tracks that can store 12 to 14 cars depending on car length. The staging cassette is attached to the wall with long bolts that thread into T-nuts installed in the layout framing on the other side of the wall, while the free end is supported by removable legs.

10

Mike Armstrong has the ultimate in hidden staging areas for his layout. Staging is in a separate room with plenty of car storage in the drawers below the lower-level tracks. The area is clean and well-lit so seeing and re-railing cars is not an issue. While many may not have the space Mike has, there may be features here that can be applied to your layout. *Mike Armstrong*

11

The east-end staging yard on Tony Koester's Nickel Plate layout is open to the aisle on the front and end, but it is dimly lit with the support members painted black to avoid calling attention to the off-stage trains. *Tony Koester*

including this area as an LDE on my layout, it immediately places it in the modern time era and location, **6**. By replicating this scene, viewers who are familiar with the Georgia Northeastern Railroad can immediately relate my model railroad to the prototype.

Staging

Another important element to consider is staging. A staging yard is often compared to the backstage area of a theater from which the actors enter and exit the stage during a performance. Our model trains can operate in much the same manner, where they enter from or exit to a staging area before or after operation on the main portion of the layout. While staging yards can be configured in numerous ways, they all accomplish the same goal—they give the illusion the model railroad is connected to the rest of the rail network and provide a purpose for our railroads.

Locating a space for staging on a small layout can be a challenge. One option is to place the staging area in an adjacent room, **7**. Trains can be made up or broken down in this area away from the main part of the layout. A staging yard operator can place cars on and off the layout from storage, thus allowing for numerous trains to be run during an ops session.

A staging area can also be on a narrow shelf or a removable cassette. This open type of staging allows easy access for maintenance and troubleshooting, **8**.

12

13

On Tom Johnson's Cass County Railroad, cars are staged on an interchange track representing a connection to the Toledo, Peoria & Western Railway (TP&W). Cars are exchanged between operating sessions with other cars stored in drawers below the layout. Note the TP&W mainline track on the right is not connected to the interchange track on the layout, as the switch is located past the area modeled. *Tom Johnson*

A small yard serves as visible staging and the interchange point for the cars on Jason Slaton's Fernandina Beach Port layout. The cars are changed between operating sessions. This provides an easy solution for staging on a small layout.

14

A car float operation provides a visible staging yard on Tom Fausser's South Brooklyn Terminal layout. The car float can hold 15 cars and provides additional operations for the crews to consider when loading and unloading. The car float must be balanced as it is being switched and idler cars are used to keep the locomotive from passing onto the car float from the dock area. *Jean Ann Fausser*

When designing my layout I chose to build a removable staging cassette, **9**. The cassette is stored under the layout when not in use and can be installed in just a few minutes. The benefit of this type of staging is that it does not take up any space in the adjacent craft room when not in use.

The staging cassette represents the interchange connection for the Georgia Northeastern Railroad (GNRR) to CSX at Elizabeth Yard in Marietta, Ga. The cassette dramatically enhances my operating sessions and allows for two trains to be staged in very little space. Without the use of the cassette, the operations on my layout would be limited. It gives the impression the main part of the layout is larger than it is by having a place for trains to go to and come from that represents a connection to the rail network.

Hidden staging is another possible option. Staging can be in a separate room **10**, behind a scenic backdrop, or inside structures that conceal it from normal view. Before an ops session, trains are made up, then staged in the hidden staging yard.

Staging can also be under the main portion of the layout and trains then use hidden track, a ramp, or helix to access the finished portion of the layout. Having adequate space between the two levels is critical for access and maintenance, **11**. This type of staging arrangement is better suited for larger layouts as a helix or ramp takes a great deal of space that normally is not available on a smaller layout.

The simplest form of staging is open staging directly on the layout. Trains can be staged on the main line or an interchange siding ready to perform their work and terminate when they return to their original starting

position. Cars are exchanged between operating sessions, **12**. This type of staging still maintains the illusion that the trains have a connection to the rest of the railroad network.

Including a small yard on your layout can also serve as an open staging area, **13**. Cars are moved on or off the layout from the yard between operating sessions, which replicates the interchange with the rest of the rail network. Operating crews can pull cars from the yard to make up their local trains and then return the cars picked up by the local to the yard to be eventually routed to locations off the modeled portion of the layout. The

EXAMPLE OF PERSONALIZED STANDARDS TABLE

There is no need to present this table in several gauges, because each modeler should select curves and track standards to suit not only his chosen gauge but also what equipment will be operated. However, for rough comparison, this table is for an HO scale railroad. Double the inch measurements for O, halve them for N, add one third for S. Turnout sizes and percent of grade remain the same for all scales.	Minimum radius	minimum length easement	minimum turnout no. (single)1	Minimum turnout no. (Crossover)	Min. turnout no. (ladder track)2	Min. track centers on tangent	Min. track centers on min. curve	S-curve min. straightaway	Max. grade on Mountain division or helper district	Max. grade on balance of main line	Min. vertical clearance3	Normal vertical clearance
Main Line – First track; passenger station tracks; steam loco terminal	24"	16"	5[5]	6[5]	6	2¼"[6]	2¼"	12"	4.0%	1.3%	3"	3½"
Main line – Freight-only	21¾"	14"	5	5	5	2¼"	2⅜"	8"	4.0%	1.3%	3"	3½"
Passing tracks; diesel loco terminal branch line	18"	12"	4	5	--	2¼"[6]	2⅜"	10"	--	2.5%	3"	3½"
Industry tracks – road	18"	--	4	4	4	2¼"	2⅜"	6"	--	--	3"	3½"
Industry tracks – city	12"	--	3	4	--	2"	2½"	6"	--	--	2¾"	3½"
Freight yard	36"[4]	--	4	5	5	2"	2"	--	--	0.5%	--	--
Freight yard switching leads	24"[7]	16"	5	5	5	2"	2¼"	10"	--	1.0%	--	--

1 Wye turnouts – No. 4 on main line, no. 3 elsewhere. Special turnouts permitted where needed; radius to match minimum curvature standards.
2 Also applies where connecting two parallel tracks at minimum track center spacing.
3 Railhead to railhead where one track crosses over another; actual minimum clearance above rail to be 19 scale feet on a least one track at all points along main line, 16½ scale feet elsewhere.

4 For appearance rather than operation.
5 Applies where main route goes through curved leg of turnout.
6 2" where no crossovers are involved.
7 To provide reliable operation pushing long cuts of cars.

15

How sharp are your curves?				
	N	HO	S	O
Broad curves	17"	30"	41"	58"
Conventional curves	14"	24"	32"	46"
Sharp curves	11"	18"	24"	35"

16

When viewing these two box cars rounding a 24" radius curve from the inside of the curve, the gap between the cars is not objectionable. When viewing the cars from the outside of the curve, the sharpness of the curve is more noticeable as the gap between the cars increases.

interchange trains are not modeled, but are assumed to have arrived or departed between operating sessions.

One final option for open staging is using a train float barge to represent the staging yard, **14**. The barge provides inbound cars for the modeled portion of the railroad and a destination for outbound cars. This type of operation is perfect for a small model railroad replicating a port railroad. The barge offers a compact open staging yard that functions prototypically and provides a rail network connection for the cars on the layout.

Curve minimums

Curves are a necessary evil on all model railroads. The question is what should your minimum radius be on your layout? Broader curves are always better

than tighter ones, but take a lot of space that could be used for other things. See "How sharp are your curves," above. John Armstrong placed model railroad curves into three categories: broad, conventional, and sharp.

The category of curves you select for your layout should be based on the type of locomotives and rolling stock you plan to operate.

Broad curves will accommodate all types of locomotives and rolling stock without modification and have

a pleasing appearance. Conventional curves with handle most equipment especially if easements are provided. On smaller layouts trains speeds are usually lower so conventional curves are normally adequate. Sharp curves are acceptable for shorter locomotives and rolling stock, but adjustments or modifications may be needed for them to operate reliably.

The personalized standards table from John Armstrong's book provides the minimum radius for main line,

17

Using an easement allows the train to gently enter the curve coming up to the bridge on Joe Atkinson's layout. By incorporating easements into the curves on your layout it improves reliability and enhances the smooth operations of your trains as they enter and exit the curves. *Joe Atkinson*

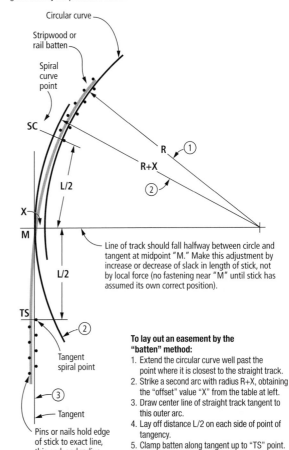

Laying out an easement or transition curve

Railroads use a mathematically generated "cubic spiral" as the transition curve or easement at the ends of a circular curve. A fair, practical approximation can be generated by the procedure below:

Circular curve

Stripwood or rail batten

Spiral curve point

SC

R ①

R+X

②

L/2

X

M

Line of track should fall halfway between circle and tangent at midpoint "M." Make this adjustment by increase or decrease of slack in length of stick, not by local force (no fastening near "M" until stick has assumed its own correct position).

L/2

TS

②

Tangent spiral point

③

Tangent

Pins or nails hold edge of stick to exact line, this end, and radius, other end

Left: When space is available, longer easements can be used as recommended in National Model Railroad Association (NMRA) Data Sheet D3b.3, with corresponding increase in offset "X."

To lay out an easement by the "batten" method:
1. Extend the circular curve well past the point where it is closest to the straight track.
2. Strike a second arc with radius R+X, obtaining the "offset" value "X" from the table at left.
3. Draw center line of straight track tangent to this outer arc.
4. Lay off distance L/2 on each side of point of tangency.
5. Clamp batten along tangent up to "TS" point.
6. Clamp other end of batten along radius "R" curve, starting at "SC" point, allowing it to assume natural curve between "TS," "M," and "SC." This is your easement. A template traced from it may also be used for any other points where a curve of this radius is joining a tangent.

SUGGESTED EASEMENT DIVISIONS FOR AVERAGE CONDITIONS		N	HO	S	O
Sharp curves	R	9¾"	18"	24"	32"
	X	3/16"	3/8"	7/16"	1/2"
	L	6"	12"	16"	20"
Conventional curves	R	13"	24"	32"	42"
	X	1/4"	7/16"	1/2"	5/8"
	L	8"	16"	20"	25"
Broad curves	R	16"	30"	42"	54"
	X	1/4"	1/2"	5/8"	3/4"
	L	10"	18"	25"	30"

18

main line freight only, branch line, and freight yards, **15**. These are the minimum standards to provide reliable operation. You'll notice if you choose a 24" minimum radius in HO scale a majority of equipment will operate reliably and should be a minimum acceptable standard for most layouts.

How you view the curves on your layout can affect design. If you only view the curves from the inside, the sharpness of the curve is less emphasized and the equipment will look acceptable running through them, **16**. If you view the curve from the

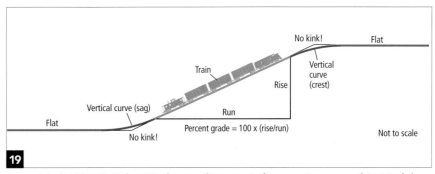

No kink!

Flat

Train

Vertical curve (crest)

Rise

Vertical curve (sag)

Run

Flat

Percent grade = 100 x (rise/run)

No kink!

Not to scale

19

An article by Van S. Fehr, "Understanding vertical curves," appeared in *Model Railroad Planning 2016*. The article describes procedures for calculating and constructing vertical grades. For good appearance, use vertical curves no shorter than the coupler-to-coupler length of the longest equipment and twice as long if possible.

Scale		N		HO		S		O	
Frog no.	Angle	RCR	R subst.	RCR	R subst.	RCR	R subst.	RCR	R subst.
4	14.25°	9"	15¾"	15"	29"	21"	39"	30"	53"
4.5*	12.5°	-	-	22"	36"	-	-	-	
5	11.4°	14"	24"	26"	44"	36"	60"	52"	80"
6	9.5	24"	30"	43"	56"	58"	76"	83"	102"
8	7.15	37"	60"	67"	110"	92"	150"	132"	200"

*Atlas "no. 4" Customline turnout is actually a no. 4.5

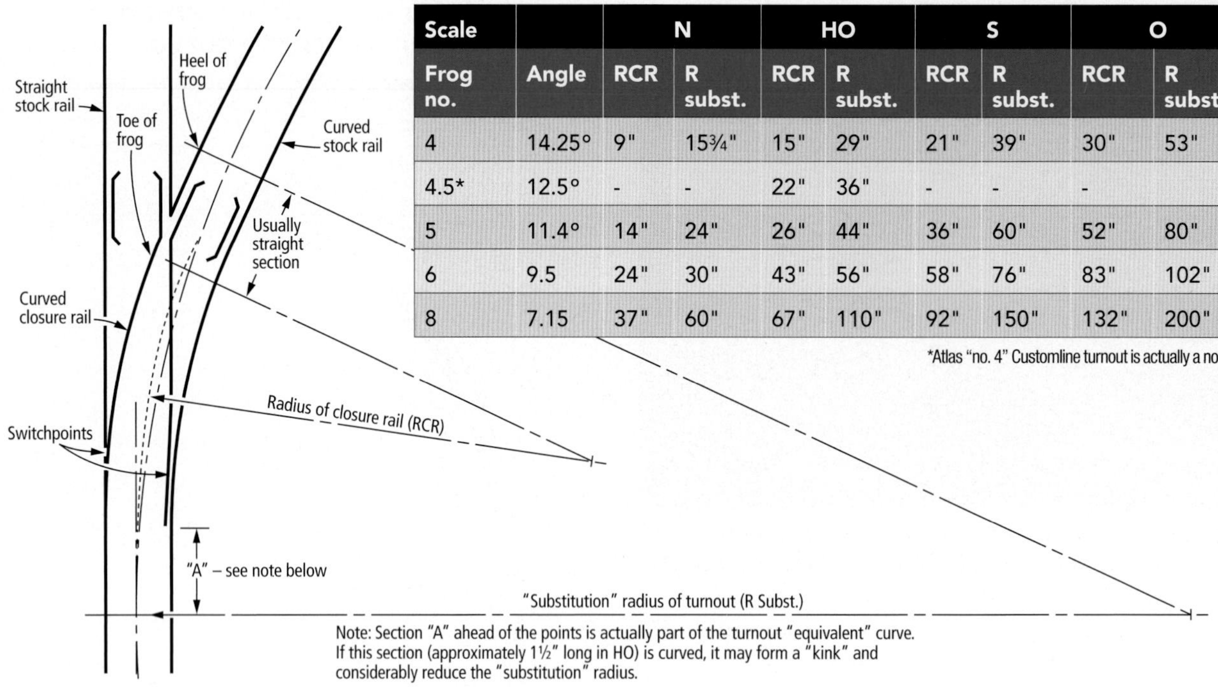

Straight stock rail

Heel of frog

Toe of frog

Curved stock rail

Usually straight section

Curved closure rail

Switchpoints

Radius of closure rail (RCR)

"A" – see note below

"Substitution" radius of turnout (R Subst.)

Note: Section "A" ahead of the points is actually part of the turnout "equivalent" curve. If this section (approximately 1½" long in HO) is curved, it may form a "kink" and considerably reduce the "substitution" radius.

The curved leg of a standardized railroad turnout is not of a uniform radius. A short section through the frog is made straight to improve the action of the wheels at that critical point and to allow the same frog to be used in right- and left-hand turnouts alike. The switchpoint is not shaped to a perfect curve because that would make it impractically long, slender, and fragile.

For any standard turnout, there is an equivalent substitution radius, as shown in the diagram, which can be substituted for the actual rail location in fitting the turnout into a section of a curve. Approximate values for substitution radii (R Subst.) are given in the table above. The most sharply curved section of the turnout is the "closure rail" portion between the points and the toe of the frog, This value (NMRA RP12 dimension 11) is also given above.

20

outside, you may want to increase the minimum radius so your trains will look better traveling around the curve.

Easements

The impact of the sharpness of a curve can be lessened by using an easement, **17**. An easement provides a gentle transition from the tangent into the constant radius of a curve and improves the appearance and operation of our trains around curves. While this may sound complicated, it really is a simple principle. One way to understand an easement is to compare it to how a race car driver enters a sharp corner. He or she starts by gently turning into the curve, then turns a little sharper in the middle and finally eases out toward the outside of the curve as the car exits. By providing an easement into a curve, this same procedure can be applied to our model railroads.

The accompanying diagram demonstrates one way to lay out an easement, **18**. The circular curve is offset the distance indicated in the chart from the straight tangent line. Where

these two lines fall at point M gives you the midpoint of the tangent length. Measure out half the tangent length in each direction and place a nail. Next, place a piece of strip wood or batten between the two nails and allow it to smoothly curve between the two points. This will provide a gentle transition between the tangent and the curve.

One easement that is not thought of as often by model railroaders is the one that occurs as a grade begins or ends. This vertical transition can easily cause uncoupling and problems during operations. Care should be taken when making vertical transitions that the grade is "eased into" and does not make a sharp abrupt change, **19**.

Turnout minimums

The next factor to consider is the minimum turnout number for your layout. The number of a turnout is determined by the angle of the frog and the angle of curvature of the diverging route. As an example, on a number 6 turnout, the rails are one unit apart at a distance of six units from the

point of the frog. It is best to select a turnout number that coordinates with the minimum radius of your curves.

In the accompanying chart, **20**, turnout radius relationships, you can see the radius of closure rail (RCR) for various turnouts. For example, if you select a 24" minimum radius curve in HO scale, a commercially manufactured number 4 turnout with a RCR of 15" would be sharper than your curve minimum and would be the limiting curve factor for your equipment. A number 5 turnout with a RCR of 26" would work well with a 24" minimum curve and actually provide a slight easement into the diverging route. A number 6 turnout with a RCR of 43" is more than adequate for even the most broad curve minimums. Handlaid turnouts can be made to match your corresponding curve minimum and provide the greatest flexibility while saving space.

Commercially manufactured curved turnouts can also be used to save some space in specific situations. Care should be taken to verify that the diverging

When planning for turnouts that are located close to a curve, it is best for the diverging route of the turnout to be on the same side as the inside of the curve to avoid an "S" curve. In situations where that cannot be avoided, allow at least one car length of your longest car from the end of the curve to the points of the turnout.

Very large industrial facilities, such as this grain facility, are sometimes too massive to be included on a smaller layout. Rather than trying to compress such a facility to an unrealistic size, it is better to omit it from your track plan. An exception is if the facility is main focus of the layout, designed exclusively around its operations. *Keith Armes*

This overhead photo of Argos Cement, foreground, shows the siding into the unloading shed has room for cars on both sides. Cars at this facility are spotted to the right of the unloading shed, then a car puller moves the cars as they are unloaded to the end of the siding on the left. It is important to account for track space on the sidings for cars to be moved at facilities where this type of loading or unloading takes place.

route is at least or greater than your selected curve minimum. Curved turnouts on the prototype are not very common, but can be a space-saver if used properly on your layout.

Simplified trackwork

Railroads are always looking for the most cost-effective way to accomplish their work. This also applies to trackwork, which is expensive. Therefore, railroads look for the simplest track arrangement to accomplish their goal. Complex "switching puzzles" are avoided on the prototype and should

also be on our layouts if we want them to look prototypical.

When considering a track design for your layout, take a look at the way the prototype railroad would go about doing it. Keep your trackwork simple and avoid complex crossovers and switchbacks. Many times railroads orient the industry sidings to face all in the same direction, which makes the local's job easier as all moves are trailing-point moves when traveling in one direction.

One special problem area to avoid when track planning is S curves.

These occur when a train is moving through a curve in one direction, then quickly switches to curving in the opposite direction. The curving back and forth leads to derailments and is usually one of the biggest problem areas on a layout. It is better to have a diverging route come off the inside of a curve rather than the outside, which eliminates an S curve, **21**. If it is not possible to change the direction of the turnout, then a length of straight track as long as the longest wheelbase of a car on your layout should be inserted between the curve and the turnout.

This prototype transloading operation takes place on a siding with a gravel road running alongside (left). A dry bulk pneumatic trailer offloads the product from the covered hopper car, then transports it to a facility that is not rail served. This type of operation is easy to model with an open area next to a siding and a dry bulk pneumatic trailer, as seen on John Farrington's Railserve layout (right). *Model photo John Farrington*

24

25

The large Farm Bureau Co-op facility on Tom Johnson's Cass County Railroad is a spot-specific industry. Covered hopper cars need to be spotted at the loading chute, while boxcars are spotted at a specific door. This type of industry adds extra work for the local crew as they must pull and spot cars in the correct order. *Tom Johnson*

26

Even small layouts need some negative space. This forest area on Tom's layout provides a visual break between switching areas on the layout and makes it feel less crowded. These negative spaces do not attract attention, but support the more visually interesting areas of the layout.

Selecting industries

If you are modeling a specific prototype, the selection of what industries to model is somewhat easier. Look at what industries are served by the railroad and also can be modeled in your space, then determine how you can incorporate them into your track plan. Very few modelers have the space to include every industry on their layout. You can select the key industries served or those that are immediately recognized as being on your prototype. On a smaller layout, sometimes the larger industries will have to be cut from your plan, **22**.

On the prototype Georgia Northeastern Railroad, the railroad serves a large grain facility. Cuts of 20 to 25 covered hopper cars of grain are delivered a few times a week. I elected not to model the facility as it would have overwhelmed the operation of the rest of the layout and would have taken the entire layout to model properly.

If you are designing a freelanced railroad, then you have many more options when deciding on what types of industries to model. Modelers should select industries that would realistically be found in their geographic area and appropriate for the era they are modeling. If possible, modelers should select industries that

take different car types to provide a variety in their train consists. Mixed trains provide visual interest and make a short train look longer due to the variety of cars.

For those industries that load or unload cars by moving them past a loading location, modelers need to provide adequate car spots before and after the loading area. The siding needs to accommodate twice the number of cars spotted there to allow room for the car movement during the loading or unloading, **23**.

An interesting car spot location that can serve a similar role of an industry is not an industry at all: it is a siding

27

Tom Patterson and Ron Long operate the Santa Fe's Alma Branch local through a vast expanse of prairie on Jared Harper's layout. Jared included large portions of "negative space" on his layout to replicate the Kansas scenery. These open spaces give operators the feeling of moving great distances between the towns.

28

Stefan Bartelski printed out a full scale mockup of his computer-drawn track plan to better visualize how the layout would look and operate. He used freight cars to test the length of sidings and placed temporary structures on the plan to check the locations of buildings. *Stefan Bartelski*

for off-spot cars. When an industry has too many cars for its location, the railroad will typically "off-spot" the cars at another siding near the industry until they are needed. This "off-spot" location can perform the same role as a "universal" industry with various types of cars being spotted there until they are moved to the industry.

Another industry to model that does not take up much space and requires no structure is a transloading location. In this type of operation a covered hopper car is spotted on a siding with easy access for a truck to hook up hoses to unload it. The truck offloads the product from the hopper car into a dry bulk pneumatic trailer and then a truck transports it to its final destination, **24**.

One option for a "universal" industry is an interchange track with another railroad. Cars on this track can be any type as they are being transferred to and from another railroad. You don't need to model a physical structure.

Spot-specific industries

A spot-specific industry is one that requires a specific car be spotted at a designated location at the industry. Some examples of spot-specific industries are chemical companies, grain industries, plastics manufacturing facilities, and warehouses, **25**. Crews typically receive a switch list from the facility indicating which cars are to be

pulled and where the inbound cars are to be placed. The cars in their consist will normally need to be sorted into the correct order prior to placing them at the facility. This adds considerable work for the local, which adds interest and time to an ops session on our layouts.

While not a spot-specific industry, a Storage-in-transit (SIT) Yard acts much the same way as a spot-specific industry. In this yard, loaded cars are stored until they are needed by a customer. Once the company that loaded the car receives an order, it notifies the railroad which specific car is to be pulled and delivered to its customer. Railroad crews must sort through all cars in the yard to find the ones that need to be pulled. Model railroaders could easily duplicate this procedure on their layouts by modeling a SIT Yard and randomly selecting a few cars that need to be pulled for an outbound train.

Siding length

Once you have selected the industries you want to include on your layout, next you need to determine the length of the sidings for each industry. Most industries in the modern era have spots for several cars rather than a single car spot that was more common in the steam-to-diesel transition era. Look at the car type required for each industry and determine the standard length for

those cars. Once you have the length and number of cars determined for each industry, multiply the length by the number of cars and add an extra ½ car length for clearance room at the head of the siding and you have determined the length of the siding required.

Passing sidings or runaround tracks need to accommodate the average number of cars in your train consist. Having a siding that is too short for most trains causes frustration for operating crews and extra moves to work around the problem.

Edit verses compress

As you design your layout, difficult choices will have to be made. Not everything you want to have on your layout will most likely be able to fit.

The general belief when designing a layout is to compress the various elements, but that leads to other problems. As distances, scenic features, and structures get compressed, realism begins to suffer. It is better to edit, that is remove or eliminate features, than try to overly compress them.

Some compression will still be needed, but structures need to look large enough to be rail-served and have some open space around each element. By leaving some open spaces, things will appear more realistic and you'll be much happier with how your layout looks.

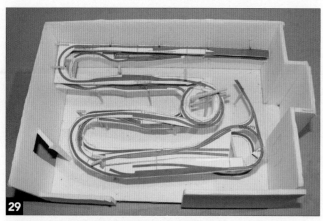

Because of the complexity of his track plan and multiple levels of benchwork, Stefan Bartelski made a model of his model railroad plan. This model allowed him to test his track plan, benchwork design, and verify the layout would fit as intended in his layout room. *Stefan Bartelski*

Temporary structures were used to test the scale of the planned industries on Tom's Georgia Northeastern Railroad. A simple cardboard box and structures from a previous layout were used. Based on these tests, Tom realized the shed structure for Georgia Metal Coaters needed to be much larger, and the brown two-story building was removed in favor of the "negative space" of a tree-covered hill.

Negative space

Until recently not much has been written about negative space, which are the areas on a layout that are visual breaks from the rest of the layout and don't contain anything to draw the viewer's interest. Negative space is similar to supporting actors in a film—they are there to fill in the scene, but don't draw attention to themselves. You'll notice that these background actors don't wear bright clothing or do anything that calls attention to themselves. The negative space on your layout should do the same, it supports and highlights the main features.

Negative space can be empty lots, parking lots, roads, forested areas, or other areas of little visual interest, **26**. These areas need to be planned for when designing a layout, they don't just happen. Layouts that have negative spaces tend to look more realistic and less cluttered than those that fill every inch of space with something eye-catching, **27**.

Computer versus hand drawn track plans

Now that we have discussed the factors to consider when designing a layout, it is time to put it down on paper. While some model railroaders prefer to design as they build, it is normally better to have a plan to be more efficient and prevent having to redo work. Plans

can be hand drawn or use a computer program. It is all up to you as to which you prefer.

If you choose to hand draw your plan, be sure to use graph paper and keep things to scale. One error most modelers make when hand drawing a plan is underestimating the amount of room required for turnouts and the correct frog angle number. By making a simple template, these errors can be eliminated.

Computer-aided design has numerous advantages as it prevents "cheating" when drawing turnouts, but the learning curve to operate the program can be steep. If you are planning to make several track plans, then learning the computer program is worth the time and effort.

Most track plans go through several revisions before the modeler is satisfied he or she has a good plan. Don't be discouraged if you are not happy with your first few designs. Once you have a plan you think will work, then look at how you would operate the layout. Imagine how each local or train would operate, where it would originate and terminate, and the type of work it would do. You can also have others look at your plan, but be prepared to hear opinions that might not agree with what your givens and druthers are. In the end, you are the one who must be satisfied with your track plan.

Full-size mock ups

If you are building a small- or medium-sized layout, one extra step that you can take before cutting your first piece of benchwork is to mock up the plan full scale on kraft paper. If you used a computer layout design program to design your layout, most have an option to print out the design full scale. While there is some expense in this process, it could save you having to redo a section of your layout if you discover it does not work on the mock-up, **28**. If your track plan is complex with multiple levels, it might be worth it to make a scale model of your plan to see how it would work, **29**.

If you hand drew your plan, you can transfer it to kraft paper using the actual turnouts and track. This will allow you to move things slightly to get the best track flow and most efficient use of space. You can also determine the scene features, location of siding and industries. Once you have your benchwork built, your plan can easily be transferred to the layout subroadbed using it as a "template." Temporary place holder or mockup structures can also be made to test the track positions and sidings before committing to the final track design, **30**. The time spent making a full scale mockup will save hours of time once track laying begins as all the bugs have been worked out in advance.

1

CHAPTER THREE

Layout construction

Now that you have an idea of the track plan you want to design, it is time to take a look at some of the import facets of layout construction. These include efficient use of space, aisle width, lift outs or removable sections, layout height, types of benchwork construction, electrical, and layout room aesthetics, **1**. These aspects need to be included in your track planning as they will have a direct impact on the operation and enjoyment of your layout.

Efficient use of space, benchwork, and layout room aesthetics

Layout construction begins on Tom's Georgia Northeastern layout. The climate-controlled layout room was drywalled, painted, carpeted, and had lighting installed prior to building the benchwork. Having a comfortable work environment made installing the benchwork more pleasant.

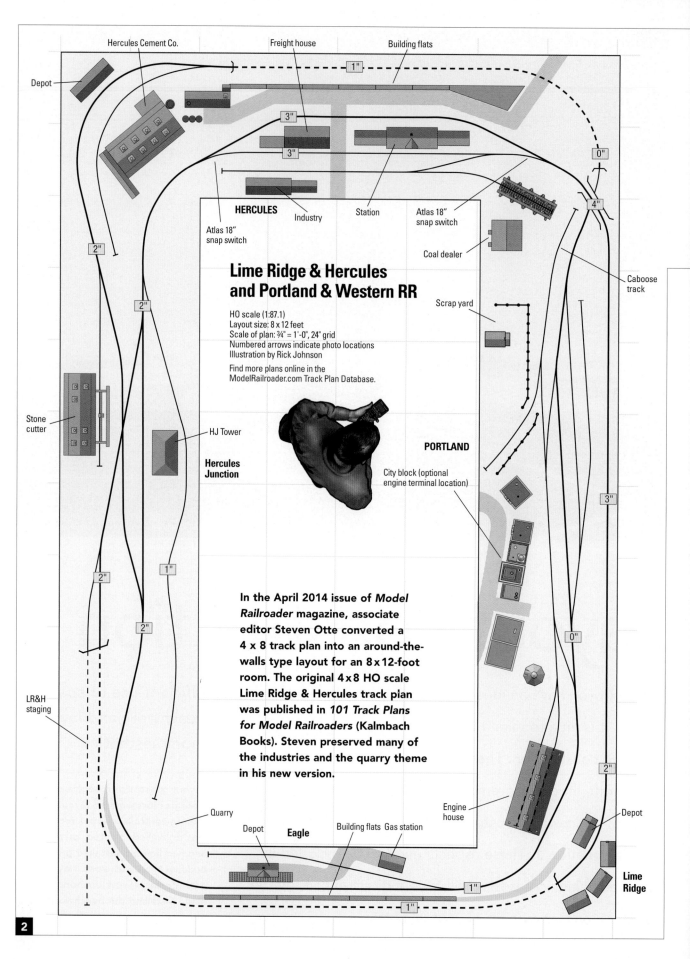

Hercules Cement Co.

Freight house

Building flats

Depot

1"

3"

3"

0"

4"

2"

2"

HERCULES

Industry

Station

Atlas 18"
snap switch

Atlas 18"
snap switch

Coal dealer

Caboose
track

Scrap yard

Lime Ridge & Hercules
and Portland & Western RR

HO scale (1:87.1)
Layout size: 8 x 12 feet
Scale of plan: ¾" = 1'-0", 24" grid
Numbered arrows indicate photo locations
Illustration by Rick Johnson

Find more plans online in the
ModelRailroader.com Track Plan Database.

Stone
cutter

HJ Tower

PORTLAND

**Hercules
Junction**

City block (optional
engine terminal location)

2"

1"

2"

In the April 2014 issue of *Model
Railroader* magazine, associate
editor Steven Otte converted a
4 x 8 track plan into an around-the-
walls type layout for an 8 x 12-foot
room. The original 4 x 8 HO scale
Lime Ridge & Hercules track plan
was published in *101 Track Plans
for Model Railroaders* (Kalmbach
Books). Steven preserved many of
the industries and the quarry theme
in his new version.

LR&H
staging

3"

0"

2"

Quarry

Depot

Eagle

Building flats

Gas station

Engine
house

Depot

**Lime
Ridge**

1"

1"

2

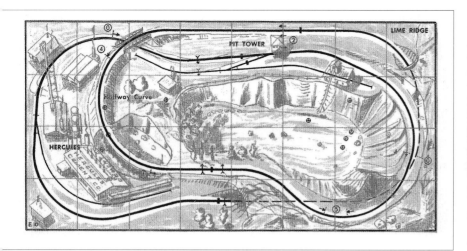

James McNab's new Hills Line layout shares family space in his basement. The layout framework base, made from Ikea shelving units, provides storage for numerous items and toys for his child. An around-the-walls type of layout design leaves plenty of space in the room for other activities.
James McNab

Efficient use of space

Numerous layouts have been designed for the standard 4 x 8-foot sheet of plywood. While it is a good way to get into model railroading and build a layout, it is not a very efficient use of space. The problem with the 4 x 8 layout is that you need access all the way around it to gain easy reach-in access. If you have a minimum 24" aisle on each side of the layout, then you need an 8 x 12-foot room for the layout, not small by any standards. If you place the layout in a corner of the room, then the 4 foot reach-in distance to the far side of the layout becomes problematic. You are also restricted to a 22" or smaller radius, and much of the track is dedicated to curved portions, which limits turnout locations and makes coupling difficult. While a 4 x 8 layout works for some, is there a better or more efficient design?

What if you take the same sized 8 x 12-foot room, and instead of placing a 4 x 8 layout in the center, you cut the lumber into shelf widths and install it around the perimeter of the room? This design will actually give you a larger layout and provide easy access to all of it, **2**. If you have a wider room, you could include a center peninsula that will give you more layout while still keeping the aisle width adequate.

With a shelf-style layout, you can design larger-radius curves and have greater flexibility with locating turnouts and industries. This type of layout can also be incorporated into a multi-use room by only using a portion of the room for the layout, **3**.

Aisle width

When you design your layout you need to consider the aisle width that is comfortable for you and your guests. As mentioned in the previous chapter, a person needs 5 to 6 square feet of space to feel comfortable in a party-like crowd. If you reduce the aisle space, the layout environment begins to feel uncomfortable. Determining what your minimum aisle space is depends on a couple of factors: the number of operators and the height of the layout.

A minimum aisle space of 24" is generally recommended to provide a comfortable operating environment. If you plan to operate the layout solo, then you can determine what a comfortable aisle space is for you and use that as your minimum. If you are going to have multiple operators for your layout, then you need to allow space for the operators to pass each other comfortably in the aisles and the aisle space should not be less than the recommended minimum of 24".

Layouts that are built at waist height allow for slightly tighter aisles as the operators can lean over the layout to pass each other. If a layout is built at shoulder height, then it becomes a little more difficult for operators to pass each other and aisle width should be increased.

On my Georgia Northeastern layout, a minimum aisle space of 28" was established, which is adequate for two operators, **4**. This minimum still allows space for operators to work, but not feel too tight. To determine this minimum, I made a mockup of

The aisle space on Tom's Georgia Northeastern layout is 28 inches. This width allows two operators to pass each other and provides a comfortable work space area for the crew without feeling crowded.

the benchwork at the proper height using cardboard boxes, and adjusted the distance between the boxes until I had a comfortable aisle space that two people could easily pass each other.

Duckunders, liftouts and removable sections

A question that comes up when designing a track plan is, can I achieve the track plan design I want without creating an obstruction to easy access? The easiest advice to give is to avoid duckunders, lift-outs, or removable sections where possible. Having a walk-in style layout where operators

5

Mark Dance built a short lift gate to facilitate easy access to the inside portion of his layout. The design is unique in that in the lowered position it is a duckunder at 4'-3". Once it is raised the clearance increases to 5'-1" creating a nod-under for most operators. *Timothy J. Horton*

6

On Tom's Georgia Northeastern layout, a removable industry is built on a lift-out section that fits across the entrance to the layout room. In its installed position, the clearance is 48" from the bottom of the lift-out to the floor, which allows operators to duck under it to exit the room. The lift-out is only installed when the industry is scheduled to be switched, approximately every fourth operating session.

7

In the May 2012 issue of *Model Railroader* magazine, Jerry Dziedzic explains how he built a self-stowing gate for his layout that was designed by Lou Steenwyk. The gate utilizes a side-mount steel drawer slide with a hinge mounted across one end. The gate lifts up on the drawer slide end and then once it clears the other end, folds down and can be lowered to its vertical stowed position. Electrical interlocks were added to prevent trains from crossing when the gate is in the lowered position. *Jerry Dziedzic*

8

Thomas Oxnard designed a swing gate to provide access to his furnace room. The gate can easily be swung out of the way for the occasional maintenance needed on the furnace. Track feeders and a Digitrax LocoNet cable run across the hinged side of the gate and have enough slack to accommodate the gate when it is opened. *Thomas Oxnard*

can easily follow their train is the ideal design and creates an ergonomic operating environment. While this type of design is ideal, what options are available if you must include a way to access the interior aisle space of your layout? This is where the duckunder, lift-out section, or removable section comes in to solve the design issue.

The duckunder is the simplest solution if your layout is high enough to allow operators to easily duck

under the layout. In these areas the benchwork can be thinned as much as possible to increase the duckunder opening height. I have found a minimum duckunder height of 48" is sufficient for most people to negotiate without too much trouble. If the height can be increased, it will make getting under the layout even easier. If the layout height is around 60" or higher, it allows a nod under which is the least objectionable type of duckunder, 5.

In areas where a permanent duckunder is part of the layout design, the addition of hand rails along the side of the area below the layout increases the comfort of operators as they move under the layout. The hand rails allow them to steady their balance and have something to hold on to as the duck down and then stand up again. If the duckunder is relatively low, a rolling chair can be used to allow guests with limited flexibility to sit in

9 A piece of clear acrylic is installed when the removable section is not in place on Tom's layout. The acrylic protects the ends of the rails from being snagged as operators pass by and prevents cars from accidentally being shoved off the layout when the removable section is not installed.

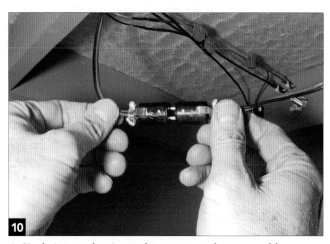

10 A Cinch Jones plug is used to connect the removable section's track power to the rest of the layout. This type of plug has different sized prongs so it can only be connected one way, keeping the polarity the same for the track on the removable section.

11 Tom's Georgia Northeastern layout was built at a height of 54". This elevation provides a comfortable height for operations and room for a collapsible workbench to be placed under the layout. During operating sessions the workbench can be folded up and stored under the layout.

12 James McNab's IAIS Grimes Line layout demonstrates you don't need a lot of depth to have a very effective and prototypical scene. The grade crossing scene is on an 8" deep shelf and the use of photo backdrops greatly enhances the depth of the scene. *James McNab*

the chair and then roll under the layout before standing up again. In all cases, the lower edges of the layout should be padded to reduce injuries if someone stands up too quickly and contacts the layout. High visibility tape can also be used to identify the duckunder and prevent injuries.

If a duckunder is not possible, the next choice is a lift-out, drop-down, or swing-gate option. Each type of removable section has its own advantages and disadvantages. If a layout removable section is only going to be inserted occasionally then a lift-out section works well.

On my layout I built a removable section to provide a continuous run

option and another industry to switch when it is occasionally installed. The removable section is constructed slightly smaller than the opening and then inserted between the permanent portions of the layout. Once in position, the section is bolted into place and the track electrical connection is made. Having a little play in the mounting bolt holes allows for slight adjustments of the removable section to align the track and achieve a perfect transition between the sections, **6**.

Drop-down or lift-up section designs are best for movable sections that will be used frequently. A hinge is installed on one side of the drop-down and the other side has a latch or

pin mechanism that holds the section in position. When the section is to be moved, the latch is moved and the section swings out of the way to allow access. These types of movable sections are best used on straight portions of track and should be kept relatively narrow to reduce weight. Scenery on these sections needs to be kept to a minimum to give the greatest clearance when the section is in the open position, **7**.

The final option is a swing gate type of movable section. In this option, the movable section is constructed much like a door with the layout track base on top of the door. Operators can move the section as easily as opening

These photos, taken on Tom Johnson's Logansport & Indiana Northern layout, demonstrate that scenes do not have to be deep to look realistic. The country scene with the power poles and the road is only 8" deep. In the second photo of the country store and gas station, it is very hard to see where the backdrop begins and the 3-D scenery ends, a tribute to Tom's artist talent. Adding trees to control the viewing angle keeps the perspective of the road correct. *Tom Johnson*

13

14

Tall structures can be an impediment to operations. If possible, taller structures should be placed toward the backdrop with the track running in front of the structures. When this is not possible, modelers should allow room on each side of the structure for easy reach-around access. Keeping structures low near the aisle permits easier access and prevents damage to the structures.

15

By constructing his benchwork framing in the garage, assembly was sped up and helped keep the layout room clean. Tom placed the cross braces on 16" centers and drilled holes for the wiring. The flat cross braces placed on the top two framework sections mount to shelf support brackets. The benchwork was painted, then carried to the train layout room and mounted to the walls.

a door and then close it once they pass through. Provisions should be made to make adjustments in the track alignment to allow for temperature and humidity changes, **8**.

In all cases of movable sections, an interlock system should be installed to prevent trains from falling off the layout when the section is not in place. The interlocks can be electrical or mechanical. If electrical power is cut off when the section is removed, locomotives equipped with stay alive capacitors need to be accounted for and the stopping section length increased. A simple mechanical solution is a

dowel that is inserted when the section is removed to create a stopping block. On my layout I use a sheet of clear acrylic bolted to the fascia when the removable section is not in place, **9**.

Power to the removable section can be provided by a stereo jack plug or a Cinch Jones plug, **10**. Both options allow for quickly connecting the electrical bus wire to the removable portion of the layout.

Benchwork height

What is the ideal height for a layout? The answer depends on the layout owner and the type of layout you are

designing. For most people the ideal height for a layout is between 48" and 54" for those who stand during operating sessions. If you choose to operate from a chair, the layout can be set much lower.

Double-deck layouts have their own unique issues when it comes to layout height. The compromise with a double-deck design is that one deck is normally below ideal height and the upper deck may be above ideal height. The space between the two decks also is a limiting factor. For those considering a double-deck layout design, Tony Koester's book *Designing and Building Multi-Deck*

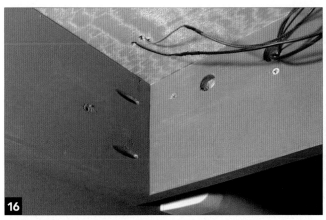

16

Pocket screws create a strong joint between pieces. A jig, purchased at a home improvement store, makes the task of drilling the pocket screw holes easy. One additional advantage of using pocket screws for the cross piece frame members is they can be unscrewed and re-installed if they need to be moved to accommodate a switch machine.

17

On James McNab's new Hills Industrial Line layout, he created a river scene by carving away the foam base. These scenic areas need to be planned for when building benchwork. The framing can be cut or lowered to accommodate the scenic feature. By varying the terrain, it prevents a "flat earth" look to the model railroad. *James McNab*

Model Railroads from Kalmbach Books is recommended reading to acquire a better understanding of what is involved with designing a double-deck layout.

Most layout operators agree that having a layout just below armpit height provides a realistic viewing angle and allows for reaching into a scene to uncouple cars or manually operate switches. If you use remote uncoupling and electrically controlled turnouts, the layout can be slightly higher and not affect operations.

The layout owner's height needs to be considered when determining an ideal height. If the layout owner is above or below average height, then the layout height should be adjusted to allow for greatest comfort for the owner. Those guests who are shorter than average can use step stools to be able to access the layout easier.

My Georgia Northeastern layout was built at a finished base height of 54". This height was ideal for me and allowed for space under the layout for my workbench and storage of model railroad supplies, **11**. Most guest operators can easily access the layout to manually operate switches and perform uncoupling with a skewer.

Benchwork width

Another factor that needs to be considered when designing a layout is the depth of the benchwork. While many consider a very deep scene to

look realistic, it comes with some very real limitations. The acceptable reach in depth that is comfortable for most modelers is between 24" to 30". At that depth most modelers can still reach into a scene for maintenance or to re-rail a car. Once the depth is greater than 30", special provisions have to be made to access those locations. Murphy's Law is in full effect in these out-of-reach areas with most maintenance issues and derailments occurring there.

Deeper scenes also require more scenery materials and can become costly when it comes time to scenic them. For a single track main line, a shelf layout can be as narrow as 8" to 10" and still provide plenty of room for scenery along the right-of-way. On James McNab's IAIS Grimes Line layout, he modeled a single track grade crossing on an 8" deep shelf, **12**.

The use of photo backdrops greatly enhances the look and increases the depth of narrow shelf scenes. Tom Johnson is a master at blending 3-D scenery into the backdrops on his Logansport & Indiana Northern layout, **13**. Scenes as narrow as 8" can effectively be modeled and look much deeper than they are by incorporating backdrops into the layout scenery.

For shelf style switching layouts, a depth of 18" to 24" is ideal for industrial or yard areas. That distance allows for several tracks and room for structural flats along the backdrop.

One final element for consideration when planning for layout depth is the height of structures or scenery features in the foreground. When possible these features should be kept low to allow for reaching over easily. If a tall feature must be placed near the aisle, it should not be surrounded by other tall structures so that operators can reach around it, **14**.

Types of benchwork construction

There are several different benchwork construction methods you can choose from depending on the track plan you select. If you design a switching layout with few changes in elevation, you can easily use a conventional open grid frame with a plywood or foam surface. Another option for a switching layout base is using a flat panel hollow core door as the foundation for your layout.

Those who design a layout with variations in elevation can use a "cookie cutter" or a spline type of layout base construction. No matter which type you choose, time and money spent in this phase of layout construction will contribute to a layout that operates dependably.

The most common type of benchwork construction is one built with conventional framing. In this method, a framework of 1 x 4 or 1 x 6 lumber is used to create a framework similar to a wood-frame stud wall, **15**.

18

The holes for the wiring runs were drilled prior to installation of the layout 2" foam base. It is much easier to drill the holes before the layout base is installed. Also note the notch in the benchwork where a small stream will be installed. A 10" wide piece of ¾" thick wood was mounted to the framing to provide a stable base for the stream.

19

Ikea's Ivar shelving units proved to be a cost effective and stable base for James McNab's layout. The shelving is adjustable and the layout subroadbed base and James' Easy DCC system and ProtoThrottle controls can be easily attached to the shelf legs. The Ikea shelving units provided a neat and clean look with plenty of storage for the layout room. *James McNab*

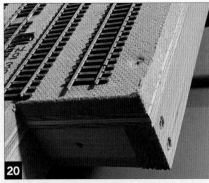

20

William Sampson used ¾" plywood for his layout base topped with a sheet of Homasote. Made from environmentally friendly recycled newspaper material, Homasote readily accepts track spikes for those who choose to hand lay their track and large sheets can be purchased for yard areas that have limited changes in elevation.
William Sampson

I have found it worth the extra money to purchase a higher grade of dimensional lumber to circumvent the issues of warped pieces of lumber that can occur with lesser grades. Some modelers prefer to use ¾" plywood cut into 4"- or 6"-wide strips for the framing to avoid some of the issues with trying to find straight and stable dimensional lumber. Following this method of construction adds the extra step of cutting the 4 x 8 sheet of plywood into the necessary strips, but it does result in a very stable piece of framing lumber.

To begin building a conventional frame, start by building a box frame to the needed dimensions. I prefer to use pocket screws to attach the pieces at the corners, in addition to wood glue, **16**. This provides a very strong and stable corner. Next, intermediate framing pieces are placed at 16" intervals. If you are not sure if they will need to be moved to accommodate a switch machine, or other component, they can be attached with pocket screws and not glued or nailed in place. If you find later that the intermediate framing needs to be moved, it can easily be unscrewed and moved a few inches in either direction, then reattached.

As you build your benchwork frame, be sure to take into account scenic features such as valleys, rivers and streams that will be lower than the base elevation. The frame can be notched or lowered to accommodate these scenic elements. By including a few of these scenic elements, it prevents a "flat earth" look to your layout and makes it appear more realistic, **17**.

Before you install the subroadbed surface, take the time to drill holes for the wires to pass through the benchwork. On my layout I drilled three holes in each crosspiece, one for the DCC bus wire, another for the Digitrax Loconet cable, and a third for the accessory lighting wiring. It is much easier to drill the holes for the wires while you have easy access to the framework than to wait until later when you will have to work from below the layout, **18**.

Recently, several modelers have discovered using Ikea's Ivar shelving units for their layout base support works very well. The shelving units allow for quick construction and provide a nice finished look and storage space below the layout. After the open shelving bases were built, framing was added to the top to accommodate the layout subroadbed, **19**.

After building your framework, the next decision is selecting the sub roadbed base. Currently there are two popular options, plywood or extruded-foam insulation board. Each has their own benefits and drawbacks.

The choice for many years has been ¾" plywood, **20**. The material is readily available at home centers and can be cut with standard power tools. The disadvantage is that it is heavy and does not allow for scenic elements to be easily carved into the surface to represent ditches along the right-of-way.

More recently extruded-foam insulation board has been used as a layout base. The advantages are its light weight, ability to be easily cut with a sharp knife, and that scenic elements can be carved into it to vary the base terrain, **21**. Some of the disadvantages are that it is messy when you use a foam shaper tool to carve out scenic features, and you can get a drumming noise transferred from the roadbed. This drumming noise is more apparent when trains are operated at higher speeds and not as noticeable on a slow speed switching layout.

A few modelers have developed a hybrid subroadbed system where they have conventional benchwork topped with a thin sheet of plywood and then a layer of extruded foam. This method reduces the drumming noise and provides a stable base that helps reduce dimensional instability.

One characteristic that must be dealt with both types of layout

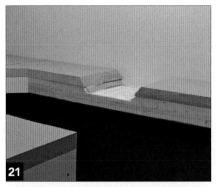

21

A layer of 2" thick extruded-foam insulation board was used as the base layer on Tom's Georgia Northeastern layout. The foam was glued to the wood framework with a foam safe adhesive caulking. Scenic features, such as this river valley, can be carved into the foam and shaped with a foam shaper hand tool, hot wire foam cutter, or a sharp knife. Acrylic latex paint was used to provide an earth colored base for the scenery. Modelers should avoid the use of petroleum-based paint as it can attack the foam. Some shrinkage of the foam is possible over time, but if it is glued to the layout base and the room is climate-controlled, the shrinkage can be minimized.

22

Two 18" wide flat panel hollow core doors were used for the yard area on Tom's old CSX Hawksridge Division layout. The doors provided a stable and lightweight base for the layout even in the harsh environmental conditions found in his Miami, Fla., garage. The doors were supported by heavy-duty shelf brackets mounted to the wall, eliminating the need for support legs.

23

Ryan Moats used a "cookie cutter" style of benchwork for his HOn3 Blackhawk & Central City Railroad. The advantage of this style of benchwork is that it easily allows elevation changes and can be cut from sheets of plywood. The 10'-0" x 11'-6" layout is based on the Colorado Central RR in the 1870s. *Ryan Moats*

subroadbed is contraction and expansion. Contraction occurs in all products, but it can cause issues if not accounted for when building a layout.

Wood expands and contracts based on temperature and humidity. As the framework and subroadbed move, they can transmit those forces to the trackwork and cause kinks. Extruded foam also has a shrinkage factor as it ages that can cause similar issues.

There are several steps a modeler can take to reduce these problems. The best way to reduce expansion and contraction issues is to maintain a consistent temperature and humidity in the layout room. In addition, leave a slight gap, approximately the thickness of a business card, between track sections at the rail joints. This gap allows for the rails to move slightly and not kink them out of gauge. Finally, the subroadbed should be securely attached to the layout framing. With extruded foam, this must be done with foam-safe adhesive caulking.

Another option for a layout subroadbed is a flat panel hollow core door. These doors are dimensionally stable and provide a lightweight flat surface for your layout. The doors come in a variety of dimensions and can be ordered from a local home center. The doors can be easily mounted to a wall using shelf brackets or placed on a base framework with legs. On my previous CSX Hawksridge Subdivision layout, I used two hollow core doors for the yard area, and they provided a very stable base even though they were in my garage, which was not climate controlled, **22**. You can also add a layer of 1" extruded foam on top to allow for some shallow scenic relief elements. This type of construction has

an added benefit of being easy to move in the future if your housing situation changes.

Another type of layout subroadbed construction is a "cookie cutter" design. This type of roadbed is similar to a conventional framing method with a flat plywood subroadbed, but incorporating either an L-girder type of base framing, or open grid framing, and using risers to elevate the subroadbed. In this type of construction, a large sheet of usually ¾" plywood is cut to the track design allowing for a few scale feet on each side along the right-of-way. Next, the subroadbed is elevated with risers above the benchwork frame. Reinforcement plates are added where

24

Greg Smith built his 18 x 18-foot Great Northern Railroad, set in 1960s, using laminated Homasote splines. The spline roadbed creates natural spiral easements and smooth flowing trackwork. Greg beveled the outside splines to form a ballast profile for his roadbed. The Homasote provided a stable base when he handlaid his track.
Greg Smith

25

Tom installed track electrical cutoff switches for the locomotive service area in the fascia on his layout. The switches shut off power to the tracks where several locomotives are stored and reduces the electrical load when powering up the layout. In areas where a large number of locomotives are stored on a layout, individual track power shut off switches should be installed.

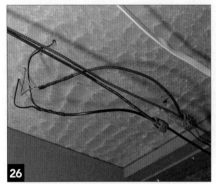

26

22AWG feeder wires are soldered together to one 18AWG secondary feeder wire. The solder joint was covered with heat-shrink tubing. These feeder assemblies were made up at the workbench, then connected to the main 14AWG bus wire with suitcase connectors, reducing the number of connections needed to the main bus. This method also kept the 22AWG feeder wires to 6" or less, reducing the voltage drop in the smaller gauge wire.

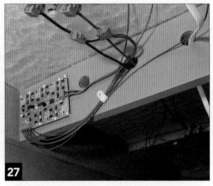

27

A Tam Valley Depot DCC Hex Frog Juicer provides power to the turnout frogs on Tom's layout. The device automatically reverses the polarity of the frog to provide power as the locomotive crosses the turnout. It is important to provide power to the frogs on a switching layout as locomotives can be prone to stalling on the turnouts due to the slower operating speeds.

28

All the Digitrax DCC system components were mounted to a pull-out shelf to facilitate easier access and installation on Tom's layout. Once the various components were installed and connected together, the shelf was installed and the main bus wires to each power district were connected to the terminal strip at the rear of the shelf. The final step in the electrical installation was plugging in all the components into an AC power strip.

two sections meet and the subroadbed is secured to the risers with screws. This type of construction is ideally suited to layouts with elevation changes or replicating tracks through a mountainous terrain, **23**.

The final option for a layout subroadbed is using splines. The spline type of construction is similar to a cookie cutter design except for the type of subroadbed installed. To create a spline, plywood, tempered hardboard, or Homasote is cut into thin strips, usually 2" to 3" wide, and then bent into position following the track design. Additional strips are added to each side of the original spline, glued and screwed to form a thickness sufficiently wide for the roadbed. The spline joints are offset to provide a smooth transition between the individual spline sections. Risers are used to elevate the splines to the desired grade. Full-size track mockups on paper are very beneficial to aid in construction and location of the spline roadbed correctly. Builders of this type of layout construction tout its smooth flowing design and quiet roadbed, **24**.

Modelers should choose the type

29 Jared Harper selected 5000K, color rendering index (CRI) 91 percent, fluorescent lights for his Santa Fe Alma Branch layout. The light fixtures are over the aisle so the light illuminates the sides of the cars and provides a nice even light for the layout. Fluorescent lights should have a CRI of 80 percent or higher to provide a good color light spectrum.

30 Tom Johnson installed LED puck lights on the ceiling in his layout room using double-sided tape. The surface-mounted lights provided an alternative to cutting holes in the finished ceiling for recessed lights and wiring. While the puck lights are off in the photo, you can see how they were installed and connected together. *Tom Johnson*

of layout framing and subroadbed that works best for their specific situation. Each method has its advantages. It all depends on your track plan and what operational goals you have for your layout.

Electrical

If you ask most model railroaders what their least favorite task of building a layout is, it usually is electrical work. While not many may enjoy crawling around under their layouts working on wiring, without it our trains would not run unless we switch to a "dead rail" type of locomotive control. *Wiring Your Model Railroad* by Larry Puckett, and *Basic DCC Wiring for Your Model Railroad* by Mike Polsgrove, available from the Kalmbach Hobby Store, are excellent books that cover DCC wiring for your layout. These books, and many others, have been written on this subject so this section will only touch on a few highlights and recommended procedures that pertain to wiring your model railroad.

Select a color code for your wiring and stick to it. Don't be tempted to substitute a different color wire with the hopes you will remember months or years later when it comes time to

diagnose a problem. For my Digital Command Control (DCC) power bus I used red and black—those two colors are the only ones used for the DCC system. To make it easier to remember when hooking up the feeders, I chose black for the rail farthest from the aisle. All I had to remember was "black to the back" when connecting the track feeders to the bus wire.

I also divided the layout into power districts and added circuit breakers for each. It makes troubleshooting easier, reduces load at power startup, and a short in one district does not affect the rest of the operations on the layout. In addition, shutoff switches were added to the locomotive service yard tracks and staging cassette. These switches keep the locomotives from drawing power when powering up the layout and prevent tripping the electrical zone circuit breakers, **25**.

I used 14 American wire gauge (AWG) wire for the main bus wires, 18AWG for the intermediate feeder wires connected from the main bus wire to the feeders, and 22AWG feeders. Using the 18AWG wire allowed me to use suitcase connectors to connect the feeders to the bus wire and keep the smaller 22AWG feeder wires 6"

long or less. Feeders were connected every 3 to 4 feet along the tracks. In many cases I connected feeders of adjacent tracks together and soldered them to one 18AWG wire, which was then connected to the main bus wire. This procedure reduced the number of suitcase connectors needed, **26**.

On a small switching layout, it is important to power the switch frogs to eliminate locomotives stalling on turnouts. Due to the slow speeds, it is much more common for the locomotive to stall when it is on an unpowered frog than when a locomotive passes over the switch points. The frogs can be powered through a turnout switch machine or a device such as a Tam Valley Depot Frog Juicer. Since my turnouts are manually lined, I selected Frog Juicers for my layout. Installation was easy. I connected the device to the DCC power bus wires, then connected one wire to each frog from the frog juicer. I have been satisfied with how well they eliminated stalling on a turnout, **27**.

All DCC system components were installed on a pull-out shelf. This arrangement allowed me to mount and wire the various components at the workbench, then install it under the

31

On Tom's Georgia Northeastern layout, he installed a combination of two different types of lights to provide illumination. The florescent lights provide a "blueish" light while the LED track lights have a warm tone to the light. When both light sources are on, it gives the room nice combination of light that works well for the layout.

32

Scott Thornton installed handrails along the fascia of his layout to provide a place for operators to rest their arms and not lean on the layout. The handrails are painted the same color as the fascia and blend nicely with the room aesthetics.
Scott Thornton

layout. The only electrical connections to be made once it was installed were the bus wires to each power district, then plug in the AC power to the outlet, **28**.

Layout aesthetics

The room and the setting the model railroad occupies must be given consideration even before beginning a layout. Many times model railroaders are in a hurry to build their layout and skip over some important aspects of the layout room. Having a comfortable and well-lit room goes a long way when it comes time to work on your layout.

If at all possible, your layout room should be climate controlled. This provides greater comfort for you and your operators, as well as keeps the layout in a stable environment that reduces expansion and contraction. It

is much more enjoyable to work on a layout when you don't have to deal with excessive heat or cold. If the train room is a comfortable place you enjoy being, it allows you to make better progress on your layout.

Having a layout space with finished walls and a ceiling will keep the layout cleaner and reduce dust. The floor also needs to be considered for operator comfort. This can be accomplished with carpeting or rubber floor mats that help reduce the effects of standing for periods of time.

Lighting for your layout needs to be planned prior to construction. Adequate electrical service must be installed and located to properly illuminate the layout. There are numerous choices for lighting including incandescent, LED, fluorescent, and string or rope lights. An electrician can calculate the load and install the proper circuits to safely power all your lighting needs. Selecting a type and color of lighting is a very personal decision, what looks too blue to one person looks perfect to another. The best advice is to experiment with your lighting options in the actual layout room and determine the type and color of lighting that you like the most, **29**.

Tom Johnson was searching for lighting options for his new layout room that did not involve cutting holes in the ceiling. While he was at a home improvement store, he found surface-mounted puck lights.

These lights could be attached to the ceiling with double stick tape and be "daisy chained" together with plug in connections from each light. The lights are LED, and powered by a standard wall plug with an in-line switch. Tom said the installation of the puck lights was easy and that they provide plenty of light for his layout, **30**.

For my Georgia Northeastern layout, I selected a combination of LED track lights and fluorescent fixtures. Using track lights allows for each light to be positioned where it provides the best lighting for the layout. The LEDs convey a "warm" light, while the florescent lights provide a bluish light. With both types of lighting on, there is a nice balance of light that replicates daylight on my layout, **31**.

Having a painted fascia adds a finished look to your layout. Even if your layout is a long way from being finished, it will look so much more completed with a fascia installed. The fascia color should complement the layout scenery colors and help a layout blend into the room. Having the fascia follow the contours of scenery provides a border and helps it blend seamlessly into the layout. This is especially important if the room is intended for other usages. To prevent operators from leaning on the upper edge of the layout fascia, a handrail can be added that gives operators a place to hold on or rest their arms, **32**, thus reducing damage to the layout scenery.

1

CHAPTER FOUR

Prototype inspired track plans

How do you select a prototype railroad to model when there are so many excellent candidates to select from? It all comes back to your givens and druthers that you decided on when you set out to build a model railroad. If you have selected to build a small switching layout, then the prototype you choose should feature slow-speed switching operations.

Looking to the prototype for layout design ideas

Genesee & Wyoming Inc. (G&W) owns or leases more than 100 short lines in 42 states and provinces in the United States and Canada. The Chattooga & Chickamauga Railway (CCKY) is an example of one of those short lines owned by G&W. Based in LaFayette, Ga., the railroad operates on 54 track miles from its interchange with the NS in Chattanooga, Tenn., south to Berryton, Ga. In addition to freight service, the Tennessee Valley Railroad Museum operates passenger excursion trains on the weekends during the summer on the line. In this photo, CCKY locomotive 1804, a former Illinois Central GP11, and 1700, a former Milwaukee Road GP9, switch cars at Euclid Chemical in LaFayette, Ga. *Keith Armes*

Tom Johnson's Cass County Railroad is a freelanced short line that runs from Logansport, Ind., north for 7 miles to Lucerne, on a former Pennsylvania Railroad branch line. The paint scheme has close ties to the Pennsylvania Railroad, especially the logo on the side of the blower duct. Tom custom painted, lettered, and weathered the unit. *Tom Johnson*

Seth Puffer developed his Puffer Bridge Line (PBL) freelanced railroad paint scheme as a tribute to the Soo Line that he grew up with in his hometown. No. 7305, an EMD SD40, was rescued from a friend's layout after a fire. The locomotive was restored, then repainted in the PBL paint scheme. The decal on the cab pays tribute to his friend's former layout. *Seth Puffer*

Pioneer Railcorp (PREX) owns multiple short lines including the Georgia Southern Railway Company (GSR). The railroad operates on three non-connected segments of railroad previously owned by the Georgia Midland Railway in central Georgia. This photo taken in Fort Valley, Ga., features PREX locomotives 3000, a GP20 built in 1960 for the Atchison, Topeka & Santa Fe, and 2053, a GP20 built in 1961 for the Chicago, Burlington & Quincy. All locomotives assigned to the GSR are painted for the PREX locomotive lease pool. This paint scheme would be easy to replicate for a model railroad based on this line. *Keith Armes*

The perfect candidate

More and more in the modern era, Class 1 railroads are selling off their branch lines and the work is being performed by short lines. These types of short line operations make a great candidate for a switching layout, **1**. There are still a few Class 1 branch lines that have a local train, but they are becoming harder to find. If you find one, you have discovered a rare jewel. Modelers who want to design and build a freelanced model railroad can also learn a lot from the prototype and can incorporate the same features to help make their layouts more realistic.

Selecting a railroad to model is a very personal choice. I have found that modelers usually select a railroad that they have a personal connection to. It can be for numerous reasons, such as they remember the railroad as a child, their family worked for the railroad, or they have always wanted to re-create some special memories they have about railroading. The more of a personal connection you have to the railroad, the more inspired you'll be to create and work on it.

Others choose to develop their own freelanced railroad. Freelancing allows for a lot of flexibility and creativity when modeling, **2**. Many times these freelanced railroads reflect a "what if" theme with an alternate version of history that allows the railroad to exist. There really is not a "wrong" railroad to model, you just need to find something that works for you and your requirements.

Performing research on railroads has become so much easier in the online era. Just type in a railroad name in an internet search engine and you'll have hundreds of photos and several websites to visit. Many times this wealth of information can become overwhelming. It is best to limit your search to a specific railroad division, geographic region, and era. Once you have those narrowed down, it is time to look for something that will fit your requirements for the space you have. If you have a small space, you'll have to understand that replicating a prototype railroad's high-speed main line operation is very unlikely, but there are other operational areas that might be a good fit for your space.

If you have decided to build a small

switching layout, you have a couple of choices—a shortline railroad or a branch line of a larger Class 1 railroad. Both options give you the advantage of being able to fit some of the railroad's operations into your limited space.

Small railroads, big picture

In the modern era, shortline railroads are an excellent choice for model railroaders looking for a unique prototype railroad to model. They typically have a small fleet of second-generation diesel locomotives and service several industries along a slow-speed rail line. These types of operations are perfect opportunities for model railroaders to base a small switching layout on, **3**.

Short line railroads usually interchange with a Class 1 railroad that gives them a connection to the rest of the rail network. Some short lines connect and interchange with two Class 1 railroads, which is a great advantage for their customers. Modelers can replicate these connections with a staging area or model the interchange yard location.

One disadvantage of modeling a short line is the lack of factory painted locomotives in the prototype short line's paint scheme. Several vendors now offer design services and custom decals for very reasonable prices, which makes modeling these railroads much easier than it was in the past. Many short line railroads use "patched out" locomotives, so replicating these units is simple project of covering over the original graphics and adding the new short line's reporting marks, **4**.

Big railroads, small picture

What if you decide you want to model a large Class 1 railroad. Can it be done in a small room? Yes, the key is you have to select a very small piece or specific operation of that railroad that can reasonably be part of a layout.

It is not reasonable to expect that you can realistically compress hundreds of miles into just a few feet and have it still look and operate prototypically. Look for a lightly used branch line or small industrial area that is served by a Class 1 railroad as a subject for

4

The prototype Pennsylvania Northeastern Railroad (PNRR) operates north of Philadelphia, Pa., on 55 miles of SEPTA-owned trackage. The railroad leases all of its locomotives from Rail Power Inc. This ScaleTrains GE C39-8 no. 8211 accurately replicates the prototype PNRR locomotive still in service as of 2020. It is not hard to determine the heritage of this former Norfolk Southern locomotive with the "patch out" paint scheme.

5

A CSX GP39-2 locomotive, no. 4306, rumbles down the Miami Downtown spur in 2009. The slow pace of the switching operation allows the engineer to talk to employees from the industry where he previously set out a boxcar as the crew passes by. The spur serves multiple industries on the line just northwest of downtown Miami. With its unique history and setting, this slow-speed CSX branch is the subject of Lance Mindheim's HO scale Miami Downtown Spur layout.

your layout. While these types of operations are getting harder to find in the modern era, they still can be found if you look around, **5**. As you move further into the past, more options appear.

Thinking it through

Now that you have some ideas of railroads that you can model, don't overlook what is in your own backyard. By choosing a local railroad, the ability to perform field research is much easier.

In addition, the opportunity to take photos can make it easier when it comes time to model structures and scenery.

As you look at railroads, think about how it could be adapted to a model railroad, and what type of operation you can have. Examine the switch jobs that the prototype performs, how often they service their customers, the variety of railcars, and the industries they serve. All these factors impact how much operations you can have on your layout, **6**.

6

Locomotives from two shortline railroads owned by Genesee & Wyoming, the Heart of Georgia (HOG) and the Georgia Central (GC), wait for their next assignment in Vidalia, Ga. Heart of Georgia locomotives 2038 and 2124 are GP38-2s, while GC locomotive 1713 is a GP9. The HOG connects to the GC in Vidalia, Ga., and interchanges with CSX at Cordele, Ga., and NS at Americus and Helena, Ga. In addition, the SAM short line heritage train operates on the line with HOG crews and locomotives. All of this variety makes it a great focus for a model railroad. *Keith Armes*

7a

While passenger trains no longer stop in Hazlehurst, Ga., the small depot between the runaround track and the main line is the office for the Hazlehurst Local G45 crew.

7b

Norfolk Southern locomotive 3291, an EMD SD40-2, sits outside the Hazlehurst depot on the runaround track. The locomotive is only a few feet off of a public road in Hazlehurst and allows railfans great access to photograph the unit without trespassing.

8

An NS service truck and a hi-rail truck are parked on the main line side of the Hazlehurst depot.

9

The stop arm is in its normal position for the Hester Industrial Lead. Crews must request clearance to move the stop arm prior to crossing the NS Macon to Brunswick, Ga., main line.

A few track plans

Let's take a look at a few prototype-inspired track plans. Each track plan is based on a prototype railroad and incorporates the basic operations on the line. You'll note in all the plans that there are no complicated switching moves or complex track arrangements, which makes them look and operate more prototypically.

The track plans are designed to fit in a spare room or bedroom and can be modified to fit your layout space. In addition, the plans can be used as inspiration for your own track plan design.

Hazlehurst, Ga., NS branch

Approximately 100 miles west of Savannah, Ga., lies the town of Hazlehurst. Railroading has always played a key role in the history of the town. It was founded in the 1880s as a depot on the Macon and Brunswick Railroad and named for railroad surveyor Col. George Hazlehurst. A second railroad, the Georgia and Florida (G&F), also operated in Hazlehurst. After the Southern bought the G&F in 1963, the line was slowly removed with the portions that serve the industries retained, and most of the main line abandoned. The Norfolk Southern (NS) currently has an active main line from Macon to Brunswick, Ga., running through town and crossing the old G&F main line in downtown Hazlehurst. Norfolk Southern has a local assigned to Hazlehurst that services the industries there, including those on the old Georgia and Florida mainline, now called the Hester Industrial Lead. The Hester Industrial Lead runs from the

NS crossing in Hazlehurst 3 miles north to Hester, Ga., and terminates at the Beasley Forest Products facility.

Local NS switch job G45 operates five days a week and works several industries including the Beasley Forest Products facility and Propex Fabrics. Norfolk Southern keeps an SD40-2 locomotive in town and the crew works out of the old Hazlehurst depot and a trailer stationed there, **7**. Routine service and fueling for the locomotive is provided by mobile service trucks, **8**. This type of locomotive service is perfect for a small switching layout as it does not require much space to accurately model the area.

The railroad still uses a stop arm gate to protect the movement of the local when it crosses the main line east of the depot, **9**. Maximum speed on the Hester Industrial Lead is 10 mph. On the prototype, the crew picks up the inbound cars on a siding southeast of the crossing and then returns to town to switch the industries. Once the crew completes its switching duties, it returns the outbound cars to the siding to be picked up by another train.

The layout is designed to fit into a 10 x 12-foot bedroom, **10**. The track plan closely follows the prototype track plan with a few exceptions. The biggest exception is that the crew will pick up and set out cars on the

northwest end of the depot instead of the southeast end past the crossing. This was done to preserve the crossover and provide adequate room to model the depot. This area also serves as visible staging, with cars being swapped out between ops sessions.

A drop-down or lift-out section is used to extend the main line and interchange track. If the layout is built

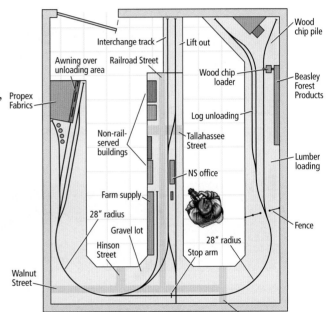

Hazlehurst

Scale: HO
Minimum radius: 28" on main
Minimum turnout: no. 6
Curved turnout to farm supply: Walthers 24" and 28"

Wood chip pile

Interchange track · Lift out

Awning over unloading area

Railroad Street

Wood chip loader

Beasley Forest Products

Propex Fabrics

Log unloading

Non-rail-served buildings

Tallahassee Street

Lumber loading

NS office

Farm supply

28" radius

Gravel lot

28" radius

Hinson Street

Stop arm

Fence

Walnut Street

Hazlehurst, Georgia
HO scale (1:1)
Room size: 10'-0" x 12'-0"
Scale of plan: 1/4" = 1'-0", 12" grid
Illustration by Kellie Jaeger

Highway 27

➕ Find more plans online in the Trains.com Track Plan Database.

10

The farm supply warehouse was no longer rail served in 2019, but it still has the rail siding in place. By backdating the layout a few years, it could easily be rail-served with boxcars loaded with farm supply products.

11

12

Propex Industries has a large facility south of town on the old Georgia & Florida Railroad line, now called the Hester Industrial Lead. The siding curving off the left is for tank cars while the siding going straight is for covered hoppers.

13

Covered hopper cars of plastic pellets are unloaded under the shed awning at the Propex facility. The pellets are stored in the silos until needed at the factory.

14

The largest customer on the Hester Industrial Lead is Beasley Forest Products. The facility receives logs and processes them into finished lumber products. Stacks of lumber are set out to dry in the sun around the large storage yard. Much of the facility could be modeled with photo backdrops or structure flats to reduce the modeled foot print to a reasonable size on a small layout.

high enough, this section could be a duckunder and eliminate the lift-out section. Aisle space is adequate at 32" between the main portions along the walls and the center peninsula. The main portions of the benchwork are 18" deep, allowing for an easy reach in depth. Turnouts are no. 6, with the turnout to the farm supply possibly being a curved turnout if required. The minimum radius is 28" to allow the long centerbeam flat cars to look and operate better on the curves.

A farm supply facility is located on a siding coming off the south branch of the line, **11**. In 2019 the facility did not receive cars, but backdating the layout a few years, the facility could receive inbound bagged goods in box cars. Including this industry adds one more facility to switch and offers a different car type than the other industries.

Propex Industries manufactures carpet backing and industrial fabrics at its facility in Hazlehurst, **12**. The facility receives covered hoppers of plastic pellets and tank cars of chemicals. The covered hoppers are unloaded on a siding under a covered awning open on the side toward the main, **13**. Tank cars are unloaded on a separate siding on the east side of the facility. The layout plan has space for two covered hopper cars under the awning and spots for two tank cars on the other facility siding.

The largest customer on the line is the Beasley Forest Products facility, **14**. The company receives car loads of logs, **15**, processes them into finished

15 Logs received at Beasley Forest products arrive on bulkhead flat cars or skeleton log cars specifically designed to carry logs. *Keith Armes*

16 The large pile of wood chips is loaded into wood chip hopper cars as outbound loads from the facility. This loading operation would be easy to model on a layout.

17 The Resolute Forest Products facility in Coosa Pines is the key industry in the industrial park area, the subject of the track plan on page 47. The facility requires constant switching by its dedicated crew, primarily shipping outbound boxcars of baled and rolled pulp and receiving inbound cars of chemicals for the paper processing operation.

lumber, then ships out the lumber on centerbeam flat cars and the chips in wood chip hopper cars, **16**. The facility is very large and has several buildings as well as an expansive wood drying lot with stacks of timbers drying in the sun. On the layout plan, a large portion of the facility could be modeled with a photo backdrop along with building flats against the backdrop.

Operations on the Hazlehurst branch line could be run as two separate switch jobs. The first job would be switching Propex and the farm supply facilities. The local would pick up the inbound cars from the siding west of the depot representing the interchange track (visible staging). The crew would switch both industries, farm supply and Propex, using the runaround track adjacent to the Propex facility as required. If the crew returns to Hazlehurst with the locomotive leading, the crew can use the runaround track in Hazlehurst to set out the cars before shoving them into the interchange track.

The second switch job would be working the Beasley Forest Products facility. Again, the crew would pick up the inbound cars from the interchange track, then perform a shove move onto the south branch. Once clear of the switch, the crew would proceed to the stop arm gate and contact the dispatcher. After the crew receives the all-clear, they swing the stop sign across the main line and proceed until clear of the main line crossing, returning the stop sign to the original position. The crew then proceeds to the facility where they use the runaround track to pick up and set out cars as required. Cars in the lumber loading area may have to be pulled and re-spotted to switch the cars at the wood chip loader. Switching this area can take some time and crews will need to plan out their moves to get the cars in the correct locations.

Once the crew completes its switching of the facility, it returns to Hazlehurst with the locomotive leading. Again, the crew will stop prior to crossing the main line and request permission to cross and swing the stop arm gate to the crossing position. After clearing the crossing and returning the gate to the normal position, the crew will proceed to clear the south switch and then perform a shove move with the cars to the interchange track. Once the outbound cars are set out, the locomotive returns to the depot and the crew completes its day.

Coosa Pines, Ala., Industrial branch line

Southeast of Birmingham, Ala., is the town of Childersburg, Ala., and the Coosa Pines industrial park. While not many people may have heard of

A trailer serves as the yard office for the local switch crew at Coosa Pines. The yard is behind the locomotive. A light tower provides illumination for the 24-hour operation at the yard. Service for the locomotives is provided by railroad fuel and service trucks. This type of operation is ideal for a model railroad as it does not require a large area or structure to model. *Tom Holley*

18

19

With the joint operation of the Coosa Pines switch job by NS and CSX, each railroad provided a four-axle locomotive. In this photo, NS 4609, a GP59, and CSX 6059, a GP40-2, sit on the lead to the small yard just across from the yard office. Due to the tight curves inside the paper facility, only four-axle locomotives could be assigned to the job. *Tom Holley*

Coosa Pines, it has played a major role in the defense of the United States. During World War II approximately 20 percent of the gunpowder used in the European Theater was manufactured there at the Alabama Army Ammunitions Plant. After the war in 1947, the gunpowder plant was converted into a paper mill. The paper plant began production in 1949. The paper mill retained the ability to return to gunpowder production within 48 hours until 1973.

Today, the 2,400 acre Coosa Pines industrial park includes a major paper product production facility, **17**, and numerous other industries. The industrial park has connections to the NS P Line and N Line on the south and the CSX Lineville Subdivision on the north. Just south of the large paper facility is a small yard where the local switch crew has an office, **18**, and an eight-track stub-ended yard. Crews pick up and set out cars at the three interchanges and bring the inbound

cars to the yard to sort and store until they are needed at the industries on the line.

Beginning in 1949 with the Southern, Central of Georgia, and Atlantic Coast Line and up until 2019, switching the industrial park was a joint operation among the railroads. Each railroad provided a locomotive, and crews from each railroad rotated shifts switching the line. In recent years, NS and CSX each had a four-axle locomotive assigned to the Coosa

Coosa Pines, Alabama no.1
Scale: HO
Minimum radius: 24"
Minimum turnout: no. 6 on main and industries
Yard turnouts: no. 5 Micro-Engineering Ladder Track System

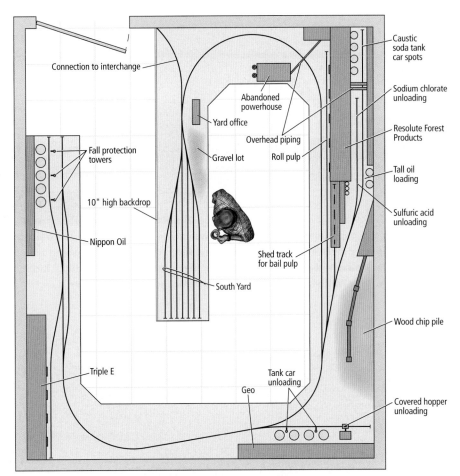

Connection to interchange

Caustic soda tank car spots

Abandoned powerhouse

Sodium chlorate unloading

Yard office

Overhead piping

Resolute Forest Products

Fall protection towers

Gravel lot

Roll pulp

Tall oil loading

10" high backdrop

Sulfuric acid unloading

Nippon Oil

Shed track for bail pulp

South Yard

Wood chip pile

Triple E

Tank car unloading

Geo

Covered hopper unloading

20

Coosa Pines, Alabama
HO scale (1:87.1)
Room size: 10'-0" x 12'-0"
Scale of plan: ³⁄₈" = 1'-0", 12" grid
Illustration by Kellie Jaeger

⊕ Find more plans online in the Trains.com Track Plan Database.

Pines industrial park due to the tight curves and track arrangement in the paper mill, **19**. In 2019, R.J. Corman took over the operation at Coosa Pines and currently provides service to the customers on the line and interchanges with NS and CSX.

The first track plan designed for Coosa Pines includes the major industries on the line and the small storage yard, **20**. The yard serves as visible staging where cars are changed out between operating sessions. This type of staging operation assumes the cars have been interchanged and inbound cars are brought into the yard by another crew prior to the beginning of the ops session. The connection to the NS interchange is represented by a track that curves off from the yard to the south. The prototype yard has no runaround track, so none was included in the track plan. The prototype crews conduct long shove moves when returning to the yard from the industrial area and interchanges.

The major industry on the line is the paper production facility, Resolute Forest Products, located along one wall of the layout room. On the prototype this is a massive facility with the rail line running in a canyon between various production buildings and pipes crossing above the tracks, **21**. Years ago, the facility was powered by a large coal-fired power plant located near the facility, which has long since been abandoned, **22**. While it is not possible to model the entire facility, I have been able to compress and edit it to fit on the layout with some of the buildings being represented as background flats or a photo backdrop. The facility has numerous car spots for tank cars, covered hopper cars, **23**, and boxcars, **24**, with many of the locations being spot-specific. The industry has

21 In this view from the cab of the locomotive, you can see the crew approaching the Resolute Forest Products facility. The tracks run in a "canyon" between the numerous structures and under overhead pipes at the facility. *Tom Holley*

22

Years ago the paper manufacturing facility was powered by a coal-fired power plant. Long since abandoned, the structure still stands today. The brick power plant could be modeled with a Walthers Northern Light Powerhouse kit.

23

A covered hopper car of sodium chlorate is spotted at an unloading area just off the main line at the Resolute Forest Products facility. The oxidizing agent is used for bleaching paper. *Tom Holley*

24

Resolute Forest Products leases 50-foot high-cube box cars for its outbound loads of rolled and baled pulp. The leased cars allow for better control of available cars for the outbound paper products.

In this view from the cab of the locomotive, the crew approaches the roll pulp loading shed on the left. The crew will switch the cars inside the shed from the far end as the siding is a trailing point move. *Tom Holley*

After leaving the inbound cars on the main, the conductor spots the locomotive to pull the outbound cars from the roll pulp shed track. *Tom Holley*

25

spots for two boxcars inside the main structure and several boxcar spots for rolled pulp, **25**. Magnetic uncoupling will be required for spotting cars on the rear sidings between the buildings. By keeping the main structure between the tracks to one story, it will be easier to see and provide a possible reach in if necessary for spotting and uncoupling.

The next industry up the line is Geo industries, **26**. The facility has a spot at the end of the siding for a covered hopper car of bauxite. The remaining two spots are for tank cars of sulfuric acid. The facility produces aluminium sulfate (alum) for the water treatment industry, shipped out by truck.

Triple E is a paper storage and distribution facility that receives and ships paper products, **27**. The facility receives rolls of paper in boxcars and stores the paper until it is needed, then ships it out in boxcars or trucks.

In addition to receiving paper from other producers, Triple E also receives shipments of paper from Resolute Forest Products. This type of operation is unusual, as normally shipments by rail cover many miles. In this situation, Triple E acts as a storage warehouse for Resolute less than a mile from the industry. Resolute's outbound pulp shipments are loaded in cars from the railroad that is the primary hauler based on the destination of the product. This arrangement reduces car hire costs for the shipper and requires the correct railroad cars to be spotted at the facility. This adds extra switching for the crews as they must have the correct car for the shipment.

The final industry is Nippon Oil, which has three spots to receive loaded tank cars, **28**. The company produces lubricants for the auto industry. The industry is spot-specific with each tank

26 A covered hopper car of bauxite is spotted at the end of the siding for unloading at Geo Industries. There are also two spots for tank car unloading at the head end of the siding.

27 Triple E is a large storage facility for the paper industry. The facility receives box car loads of paper at a side loading dock and stores them until needed. The paper can be shipped by truck from the loading dock on the street side or loaded back into boxcars for shipment to customers. The structure could be modeled with Pikestuff kit components.

28 Nippon Oil and Energy receives tank cars of petroleum products at spot-specific unloading racks on the side of the facility. The yellow towers in the right photo arching above the siding are fall protection for the workers at the facility when accessing the top of the tank cars.

car required to be spotted at a specific unloading spot based on the product it is carrying. On the prototype, the siding to Nippon Oil is a trailing point siding, but it had to be changed on the track plan to fit the space. To spot cars at Nippon requires a runaround move on a passing siding, which has been included on the track plan adjacent to the facility.

Operating sessions can be conducted with two switch jobs—the primary one is Resolute Forest Products. The second switch job is working all the other industries. The crew begins its day sorting cars from the yard into the consist for the paper industry. The cars need to be blocked in order to simplify moves at the paper facility. Once it has all the inbound cars, the crew departs north to the paper facility. The top priority when switching the paper mill is switching

out the roll pulp boxcars at the facility. Using a switch list, the crew pulls the outbound cars and sets out the inbound cars. Some cars may need to be moved and then re-spotted to access cars behind them on the sidings. After switching the industry, the crew conducts a shove move back to the yard with the conductor providing point protect. Experienced crews will place a car (usually a tank car or covered hopper) on the point end that makes it more comfortable for the conductor to ride on for the shove move. Once they return to the yard, the crew will sort the cars into the appropriate yard tracks based on the railroad that they will be interchanged with.

The second switch job will be much like the first, except the crew will sort the cars for the other three industries from the yard. Next, the crew will work

its way up the line switching each industry as required. The runaround track at the end of the line will need to be used to switch Nippon Oil. After switching the industries, the crew will make a long shove move back to the yard, replicating the procedure used on the prototype. Finally, the crew will sort the outbound cars into the appropriate yard tracks, then complete its day tying down the locomotive outside of the yard office.

Coosa Pines, track plan 2

Coosa Pines track plan no. 2 is designed for a shared-space layout room, leaving plenty of room for a bed or workbench in the room, **29**. The track plan eliminates the yard and the large paper industry, but does include a couple of industries that were not included on the first plan. This is where decisions have to be made as to what to include and what to edit out. Eliminating the yard and paper industry allows for a more realistic-looking layout in the limited space available. Two additional industries on this track plan, Hawk Plastics and the Tennessee Team track, are located north of Nippon Oil so they were not included on the first plan. Hawk Plastics produces PVC pipe and receives plastic pellets in covered hopper cars, **30**. The Tennessee Team track was used to bring in long steel girders when a highway construction project was underway, but can also be used as a transloading location if desired, **31**.

Operating sessions on the Coosa Pines no. 2 are much simplified from the first plan. The operating session begins with the train staged on the main line in front of Geo Industries. The crew works its way up the line switching each industry. Many of the industries are spot-specific, so that adds additional time and work for the crew. Once the crew reaches the end of the line, it uses the Tennessee Pass team track to run around the consist to switch Hawk Plastics. After completing its switching duties, the crew can head back down the line with the locomotive leading, or make a shove move to return to the starting position. Once back in position, the train can be restaged and another ops session started if desired. While much smaller than the first track plan, plan no. 2 still offers lots of switching and hours of operating fun.

No matter which Coosa Pines track plan you choose, there will be plenty of operations. Tom Holley, long-time NS engineer on the Coosa Pines switch job said, "It's pretty good switching. It just has a lot of cuts in it." Making cuts and switching cars what it's all about on this railroad line.

Soo/Milwaukee Road Hiawatha Elevator District

Minneapolis, Minn., the twin city to Saint Paul, is home to several unique railroading jewels. For the Milwaukee

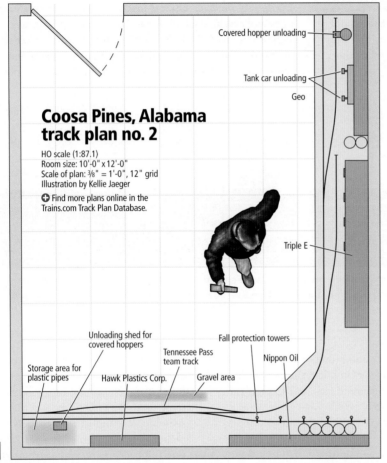

Coosa Pines, Alabama track plan no. 2

HO scale (1:87.1)
Room size: 10'-0" x 12'-0"
Scale of plan: ⅜" = 1'-0", 12" grid
Illustration by Kellie Jaeger

➕ Find more plans online in the Trains.com Track Plan Database.

Covered hopper unloading

Tank car unloading

Geo

Triple E

Unloading shed for covered hoppers

Fall protection towers

Tennessee Pass team track

Nippon Oil

Storage area for plastic pipes

Hawk Plastics Corp.

Gravel area

29

Coosa Pines, Alabama no. 2
Scale: HO
Minimum radius: 24"
Minimum turnout: no. 6

A covered hopper car of plastic pellets is spotted on the siding for Hawk Plastics. The facility makes various types and sizes of plastic pipes.

30

31

It has been awhile since the Tennessee Pass team track has seen any action. The location was used to offload construction materials for a highway project several years ago. With a little modeler's license, the track could be used for a transloading operation on a model railroad.

32

The General Mills Elevator facility on the left and the ADM Atkinson Mill on the right create a concrete canyon that Hiawatha Elevator District trains operate in. The mills were built along the Milwaukee Road line that ran from Chicago to Minneapolis. *William Sampson*

Road, three of those would be the Southtown Yard, the 29th Street depression (commonly known as "The Ditch"), and the Hiawatha Elevator District.

Directly south of Minneapolis was the Southtown Yard. It fed the passenger station downtown, an auto unloading area, and had its southern yard throat crossed by a heavily traveled east-west corridor. That track-cutting corridor itself led west to a unique stretch of track known as "The Ditch." The Milwaukee Road decided to drop the railroad thoroughfare below street level to allow for trains to come and go without disrupting city streets. As unique as that was, the southern direction from Southtown Yard may be the most interesting as it led to an area crowded with industries. This area of Minneapolis had various industries that supplied the city with flour, cement, and lumber, which earned it the nickname "Hiawatha Elevator District," **32**.

Because of its distinctive blend of industries in a compact area, William Sampson designed a track plan and modeled the Hiawatha Elevator District with a small bedroom-sized switching layout. He selected the 1985 to 1986 time period, as it was the beginning of the merger of the Milwaukee Road into the Soo Line. This allows him to operate locomotives painted in both railroads' paint

schemes. In addition, all three jewels were still active, Southtown Yard had not closed yet, "The Ditch" was being used, and the Hiawatha Elevator District was thriving.

The layout room is a guest room in the basement with a typical 10 x 12-foot area. William and his family did not plan to use it very often for guests, so he installed a Murphy bed. The bed stays folded up out of the way most of the time and can be pulled down when needed. This allows for a model railroad to fit nicely along two walls in the room. To design the track plan, William obtained area maps of the Hiawatha Elevator District from the Minnesota Department of Transportation that were originally done by North States Power in 1963, **33**. To keep the room with an open feeling and allow for the Murphy bed to fold down, William designed a 10 x 12-foot "L" shaped layout with 13"-deep shelves along two walls.

Referring to the aerial survey map, William selected industries that would allow him to build them close to full scale. On a building like the Minneapolis Seed Company, **34**, the structure will be 4 to 5 feet long in HO scale. The height of the silos at the Cargill elevator, **35**, are a towering 83 HO scale feet, as compared to the standard 64-foot HO scale Walthers silos kit. Building the silos at the prototype height will create

an impressive structure. These large industries are what drew William to model this area in a room that is only 10 x 12.

Realizing it is not possible to fit everything into his space, William decided to selectively compress and edit the prototype into a manageable size for a shelf layout, **36**. At certain points, the corridor could reach as wide as 8 tracks across. If one includes the industry tracks, you could be counting up to 10 tracks. With a shelf only 13" deep, the number of tracks was cut down to five as a maximum. This allowed for comfortable track spacing and room for building flats to fit against the wall. The area between 39th to 40th streets was omitted from the plan, as there were no rail-served industries in that block.

Most of the focus of the layout was directed toward the eastern side of the tracks, which is the wall side in the guest room, and allows for flats to represent the industries. These industries include the Minneapolis Seed Company and Cargill elevator. The western side industries had to be addressed for switching. The solution was to have open-sided flats, which could have the interiors detailed. That allows for visual interest and identification of the industry being served on the aisle side. These industries include the ADM Nokomis Mill and L.S. Donaldson Warehouse.

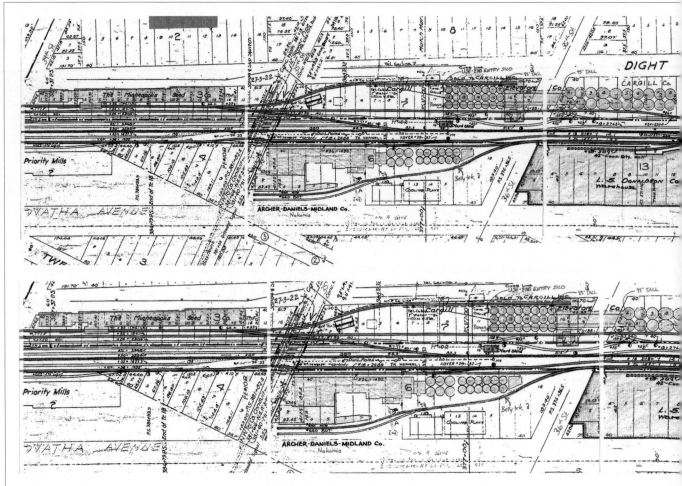

William used copies of the Hiawatha Elevator District survey, top, originally done by the Northern States Power Company in 1963, to plan his layout. These survey maps indicated all the industries and track arrangement for the area. With these maps, William selected the tracks he needed and eliminated others that did not enhance his operations. In addition, the maps provided dimensions for the structures and industries, which helped with layout planning. *William Sampson*

William highlighted the tracks he wanted to replicate on his model railroad, then rearranged the aerial survey maps into his L shaped track plan. Using this method gave William a very realistic track plan and arrangement of the industries.
William Sampson

33

As the track plan turns the corner on generous 36" and 38" radius curves, William used modelers' license to accommodate the space better. He decided to flip-flop two blocks. The one that houses the General Mills and ADM Atkinson Mill will migrate south slightly, **37**. Then Hiawatha Lumber and Freseman Manufacturing will move north, utilizing the space in the corner for the lumber yard. This also opens up for a better representation of an iconic crossover that feeds General Mills. This takes us to the end of the line where we have served eight industries on a 22-foot length of the Hiawatha Elevator District.

An operating session on the layout begins with the crew picking up inbound cars from the main line and other tracks in front of the Minneapolis Seed Company representing Southtown Yard. The crew will sort its cars into the proper order for the local switch job. Next, the crew will work all the trailing point industries as it proceeds south. Once it reaches the end of the line, it cuts the locomotive off from its consist and pulls the cars from the facing point industries. After the outbound cars have been pulled, the crew uses the long runaround track to access the cars needed for the setouts. The

crew makes a final stop at the Cargill elevator to switch the cars there before heading back to the interchange track at Southtown Yard. The Cargill elevator will be serviced by an EMD SW1 to move the cars once they are spotted at the facility. Typical locals of 8 to 10 cars are planned for ops sessions, with the possibility of additional cars that would make an ops session more challenging. A one- to two-hour operating session is possible with this compact layout.

Georgia Northeastern Railroad
Located just north of Atlanta in the foothills of the Appalachian

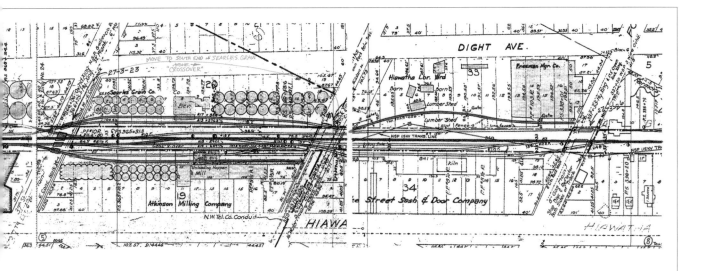

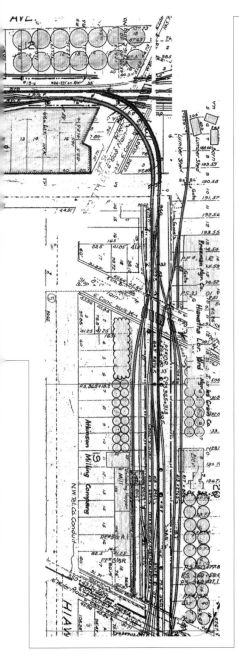

The Minneapolis Seed Company received shipments of seeds by rail and stored them in bins inside the structure. A fire in 1930 destroyed the original structure built in 1908, which was then replaced by the current brick and concrete structure. *William Sampson*

34

35

The Cargill Elevator, on the left side of the photo, was one of the major customers on the Hiawatha Elevator District line for many years. On the right, slightly down the tracks, is the LS Donaldson distribution warehouse, for a department store that grew to be one of the major retail chains in the Twin Cities. The small structure in the center of the photo is currently the Minnesota Transfer Railroad Yard Office. *William Sampson*

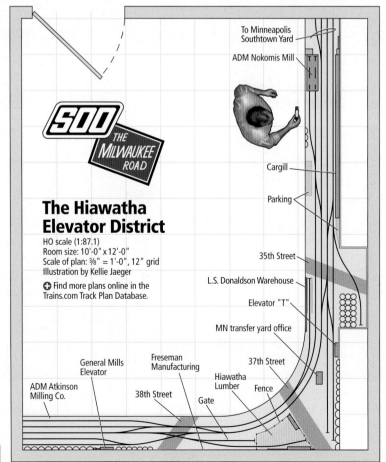

SOO
THE MILWAUKEE ROAD

The Hiawatha Elevator District

HO scale (1:87.1)
Room size: 10'-0" x 12'-0"
Scale of plan: ⅜" = 1'-0", 12" grid
Illustration by Kellie Jaeger

⊕ Find more plans online in the Trains.com Track Plan Database.

To Minneapolis Southtown Yard
ADM Nokomis Mill
Cargill
Parking
35th Street
L.S. Donaldson Warehouse
Elevator "T"
MN transfer yard office
37th Street
General Mills Elevator
Freseman Manufacturing
Hiawatha Lumber
Fence
ADM Atkinson Milling Co.
38th Street
Gate

36

Mountains, the Georgia Northeastern Railroad (GNRR) operates on a nearly 100-mile-long segment of the Louisville & Nashville "Old Line" from Marietta, Ga., to Copperhill, Tenn. Classic EMD power still works the steep grades on the line that winds its way into the mountains from a connection with the CSX Western and Atlantic Subdivision at Elizabeth Yard in Marietta, **38**.

The GNRR serves numerous customers along the line, including metal coating, **39**, concrete, **40**, lumber and building materials, **41**, grain, chemical plants, **42**, plastic manufacturing, aircraft components, and marble industries. A small locomotive service facility in Tate, Ga., provides repairs and service to keep the all-EMD fleet operating, **43**.

After researching the prototype GNRR, three key areas of the railroad were identified that I wanted to model in my track plan. These areas included an industrial area around Marietta, the yard and locomotive service facility in Tate, and finally the marble industries in Marble Hill, **44**.

The layout plan placed the key areas along the two longer walls of the layout room and the peninsula. Scenic breaks between each section were included to give crews a feeling of traveling a greater distance between each area.

The scenic areas are the bridge over the Etowah River and the trestle over Long Swamp Creek, **45**. By focusing on the three key areas it allowed me to edit the prototype into manageable sections while eliminating the need to include every industry on the prototype in my track plan, **46**.

The layout features a removable industry across the entrance to the layout room. This industry is only installed when the facility is scheduled to be switched. The removable section

---

Hiawatha Elevator District

William Sampson
Scale: HO
Minimum radius: 36"
Minimum turnout: no. 6

Looking south from 37th Street, a Trackmobile works the north end of the ADM Atkinson Mill. As of February, 2020, the facility is one of the few mills still in operation in south Minneapolis. The facility operates 24 hours a day, and produces 1 million pounds of flour a day.

William Sampson

37

Moving south one block and looking north, the ADM Atkinson Mill is on the left, and the General Mills Elevator is on the right. Numerous industries tightly packed along a major rail corridor led William to select this area for his layout. Modeling the Hiawatha Elevator District provides plenty of operations on a small layout. *William Sampson*

38

The Georgia Northeastern Railroad (GNRR) interchanges with the CSX's Western and Atlantic Subdivision at Elizabeth Yard in Marietta, Ga. The GNRR was purchased by Patriot Rail in 2015 from Wilds Pierce, who had owned the railroad since 1989. The CSX main line is in the foreground with the GNRR local crew stopped short of the yellow clearance markers on the yard track. *Keith Armes*

39

Georgia Metal Coaters receives loads of steel in coil cars. The local crew must pull and spot the cars inside the facility accessed through an overhead rolling door.

can also be used as a continuous run for an open house display or to break-in a locomotive.

While the layout is very compact, it features lots of operations. Currently there are three separate switch jobs on my layout, the North Local, the Marble Hill Turn, and the Elizabeth Yard Turn, replicating those same jobs on the prototype. The switch jobs can be run in sequence, or for those operating sessions where there are four operators, the North Local and Marble Hill Turn can be run simultaneously by the two-person crews.

The North Local begins in staging, which represents Elizabeth Yard, with

the cars blocked in industry order from south to north. The crew departs the yard northbound and switches the industries in Marietta up to Dow Chemical. Normally the crew switches the trailing-point industries first, then uses the runaround track in Marietta to run around the local's consist and switch the remaining industries. Once it has finished its switching duties, the

Argos Cement receives loads in two-bay covered hopper cars. The cars are unloaded in the large shed, then the cement is transferred using the bucket conveyor up to the storage silo above the truck loading shed.

40

41

The Capitol Materials facility in Marietta receives lumber and building supplies on centerbeam flat cars. The facility has a large paved area around the siding to allow forklifts to easily unload the products. Materials are stored inside the warehouse or on lumber racks around the perimeter of the facility.

42

A spot-specific industry, Dow Chemical, receives tank cars of products that must be spotted at specific unloading racks on the single siding at the facility. This type of operation requires additional work by the local crew to pull and re-spot cars as necessary to switch the facility. *Scott Chatfield*

crew returns to staging. Switching the industries in Marietta can take about an hour or more to complete.

The Marble Hill Turn begins in Tate with the crew picking up its locomotive from the service facility, then, using the switch list, it sorts the cars needed for its train from the cars in Tate Yard. Once it has its cars, the crew departs the yard and heads to Marble Hill to switch the industries there. The switching in Marble Hill can be a little challenging as there is limited room on the runaround track, and the tail track can only accommodate the locomotive. Once the crew has switched out the cars at the marble industries, it heads back to Tate Yard to set them out in the yard as indicated on the switch list.

The third switch job, the Elizabeth Yard Turn, takes the loaded cars from Tate Yard and sets them out on the staging cassette representing Elizabeth Yard and the interchange with CSX. The crew starts its work by picking up its locomotive from the engine service facility, then sorting the cars needed for the train from the cars in Tate Yard. Once it has its train assembled, EOT inserted in the last coupler, and a simulated brake test completed, the crew departs to staging. Just prior to entering staging, the crew sets its cars

Above left: A trio of GNRR locomotives waits for their next assignment outside the locomotive service facility in Tate, Ga. The GNRR all-EMD fleet features classic power acquired from various railroads across the United States.

Above right: Georgia Northeastern Railroad locomotive no. 2000, a GP38-2, is parked under the sand tower at the locomotive service facility. The facility has fuel, oil, and sand service for the locomotives on one siding that leads to the service building. The two-bay service structure in the background provides a covered space for routine service, and has major overhaul capabilities to keep the fleet operating.

43

The Georgia Marble quarry has been in business since 1884 and provided the marble for many statues and monuments in Washington, D.C. The facility ships large marble slabs, like those seen in this photo, and marble chips from the facility in Marble Hill, Ga.

In this photo of the Georgia Marble facility, you can see the quarry pit where the marble has been cut and removed. This specific quarry location is now inactive and the mining has been moved to a new location at the property.

44

off in Marietta, then pulls the empty cars needed for the return trip from the staging cassette. The crew then uses the runaround track in Marietta to run around the inbound consist, then shove it into the open staging track. Finally, once it has its train reassembled, the crew returns to Tate and sets its cars off in the yard.

By running these three jobs back to back, a two- to three-hour operating session is possible for two operators. Guest operators are always amazed how much operations can be held on a layout in less than a 100 square foot layout room.

45

The Marble Hill Turn Job, led by GNRR no. 6576, an ex-B&O GP9 built in 1958, crosses Long Swamp Creek Bridge on its way to the Imerys facility to set out a covered hopper car. The bridge support piers are discarded blocks of marble.

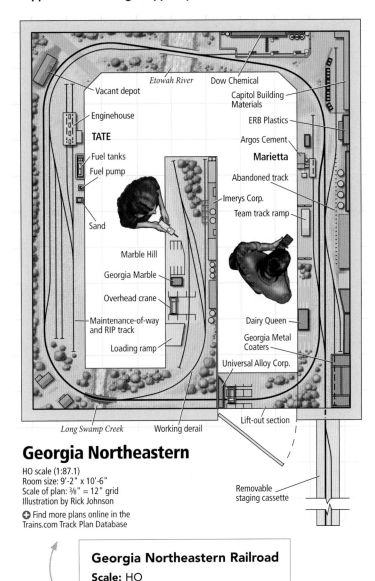

Georgia Northeastern

HO scale (1:87.1)
Room size: 9'-2" x 10'-6"
Scale of plan: 3/8" = 12" grid
Illustration by Rick Johnson
⊕ Find more plans online in the
Trains.com Track Plan Database

46

Georgia Northeastern Railroad
Scale: HO
Minimum radius: 24"
Minimum turnout: no. 6

CMEX
110652

CAUTION
NO SIDE LADDER

1

CHAPTER FIVE

Prototype operations

Prototype rules and procedures that can be applied to model railroading

Safety is top priority on the railroad. The conductor, wearing his high-visibility vest, rides the side of the covered hopper car, providing point protection for the shove move. In addition, he has his hand on the radio to communicate with the engineer and safely guide the movement. Note the brake stick hung on the ladder rung on the end of the car and the End-of-Train device attached to the side of the coupler.
Keith Armes

Prototype railroad operating rules can be summarized in three words: safety, safety, safety. Safety for the railroad employees, safety for the public, and safety for the train and its cargo, **1**. While specific rules may be slightly different from one railroad to another, the overriding theme is the safe operation of the train. In this chapter we'll cover some of the important rules and procedures railroads follow and discuss how they can be applied to our model railroad operating sessions.

The Operating Rule Book and Timetable are two documents that every train crew employee on the railroad must have in their possession while on duty. The Timetable provides updates and special instructions in effect at the time the timetable is issued.

GEORGIA NORTHEASTERN RAILROAD

TRAIN MESSAGE 031714GM1#13

TO: ALL GNRR Transportation, Maintenance of Way Staff and BLRX Train Crews

EFFECTIVE DATE: March 17, 2014, 09:30

FROM: TRAIN DISPATCHER

RE: Slow Order Terminated / Keithsburg Block

The Slow order has been lifted in the Keithsburg block from MP449.0 to 450.7 as per the GNRR Track Inspector / Maintenance of Way department.

This message supersedes train message 021114GM1#8.

This copy of a Georgia Northeastern Train Message provides information to the crews of special instructions or conditions in effect the date it was issued, in this case lifting a slow order that was in effect in the Keithsburg Block. Train crews must have copies of these bulletins or messages in their possession while on duty.

Railroad operation rule book

One of the first documents that a new railroad employee receives is a railroad operating rule book. This rule book must be accessible by the employee while on duty. Updates and special instructions to the rule book are provided in a timetable with a number and the date the timetable was placed in effect, **2**. Those employees whose duties are affected by the timetable must have a copy of the current issue of the timetable with them.

Additionally, bulletins can be issued which supersede instructions in the timetable and any rule with which such bulletins may conflict. These bulletins outline special issues or procedures of a temporary nature that affect the operation of trains, such as a stop and flag order for a grade crossing signal being placed out of service until it is repaired, or a slow order for a section of track, **3**. Employees are required to check for new bulletins at the beginning of each tour of duty and must maintain a copy of the current bulletins in effect and have them accessible when working.

Copies of railroad rule books can be found on online auction sites and at train shows. These or a copy of the General Code of Operating Rules (GCOR) for railroads make a good guideline for developing rules for operating our model railroads.

While the prototype rule book can be quite extensive, model railroaders can select the specific rules that apply to their railroads and consolidate them into a handout guest operators can be given when they arrive to operate the layout. By presenting guests a rule book on how to operate your model railroad, it gives them a framework to operate and understand how the layout owner wants to run his or her railroad.

Use of signals

For many years railroads have used hand and horn (whistle) signals to communicate between train crew members. With the advent of radios, some of this type of communication has been reduced, but modern-day train crew members still use hand signals in many situations. Crews must decide in advance of any operational period the type of signaling system being used and understand the meaning of each signal. Whether you model the transition period or modern-day operations, the signals described here from prototype rule books and can be applied to your layout operations.

GEORGIA NORTHEASTERN RAILROAD OPERATING RULES Effective March 1, 2010	
HAND, FLAG, AND LANTERN SIGNALS	
SIGNAL INDICATION	**HAND OR FLAG MOTION**
Stop	Swung at right angle to the track.
Reduce speed	Slight horizontal movement at arm's length at right angle to the track
Proceed	Raised and lowered vertically.
Back	Swung vertically in circle at right angle to the track.
Apply air brakes	Swung horizontally above the head at right angle to the track, when equipment is standing.
Release air brakes	Held at arm's length above the head when equipment is standing.
Stop	Any object waved violently by anyone on or near the track.

Hand signals are used by the railroad for communication between the train crew members. The hand signals must be given clearly and where they can be seen by the engineer. If at any time the engineer loses sight of the crew member providing the hand signals, the movement shall immediately be stopped.

This Norfolk Southern switch crew is working to safely switch the cars in the yard. The crew members are wearing their high-visibility safety vests and are positioned so they can be easily seen by the engineer. The crew members will guide the engineer to a coupling using hand signals or radio communication. Working in a yard is a very dangerous job and the top priority is always safety for the crew members. *Keith Armes*

HORN SIGNALS

The prescribed signals are illustrated herein, with "O" showing short sounds, and "–" showing long sounds. Those signals marked with an asterisk must be sounded where applicable. Those signals not marked with an asterisk convey information to employees and must be used when voice communication is not available.

SOUND	SIGNAL (HORN) INDICATION
a) O	Applying air brakes
b) – –*	Proceeding
– –	Releasing air brakes
c) O O*	Acknowledging any signal not otherwise provided for
d) O O O*	Backing up
e) – – O –*	Approaching public crossings at grade, tunnels, yards, or other points where men may be at work and when passing the rear of freight trains
f) Succession of short sounds	Warning to people and/or animals

The horn signal chart indicates the proper signal to be given for each type of movement or action. These signals are used to notify crews working in the area that a movement is about to occur, the brakes are being applied, or released.

In the accompanying chart, **4**, some of the most common hand or flag signals are listed. Hand signals must be given sufficiently in advance to permit compliance and given from a point where they can be seen clearly, **5**. If there is any doubt as to the meaning of a signal or the employee giving the signal disappears from view, the movement must be stopped immediately. Hand signals to the engineer must be given to correspond to the direction in which the engine

is headed. Model railroad crews can use hand signals to prototypically communicate between crew members during operating sessions. By using hand signals, it adds time to the switching operations as the crew has to allow time for the hand signals to be received and acted on.

Most model railroaders are familiar with the required two long, one short, and one long horn signal given by trains approaching a grade crossing, but there are many other horn signals that

can be applied to an operating session. The horn signal chart, **6**, indicates the appropriate signal for each movement or procedure. The locomotive horn signals required for Proceeding and Backing Up do not apply after momentary stops in continuous switching.

The locomotive bell is another signaling device that provides a warning that a locomotive is about to move, except after momentary stops in continuous switching movements. It must be also be rung while approaching and passing stations, public crossings at grade, while moving through tunnels, and when approaching persons on or around track structure.

By incorporating some of these signals into an operating session it will enhance the realism and replicate the prototype procedures. Engineers operating on your model railroad should be encouraged to use the applicable signal, horn and or bell, when appropriate.

Headlights and ditch lights

The Georgia Northeastern Railroad Rule Book specifies that "The headlight must be displayed 'bright' on the leading end of every train by day and night." There are a few exceptions as to when it may be extinguished.

1. When a train is standing to be met or to be passed by another train in signaled territory.

2. When a train is standing on a track other than a main track, or

3. On the end coupled to cars.

The headlight must be dimmed under the following conditions, except when approaching or passing over a public crossing at grade:

1. At yards where switching is being done

2. Approaching stations where passenger stops are to be made

3. When standing close behind another train

4. While standing on a main track in non-signaled territory, awaiting arrival of an approaching train that is to take the siding

5. When approaching and passing the head-end and rear-end of a train on an adjacent track

7

8

This CSX locomotive has its headlight on bright and the ditch lights are illuminated as it passes through a public grade crossing. The locomotive struck a car that was parked too close to the railroad right-of-way. Note the reaction of the conductor with his hands on his head when he realized the locomotive handrail hit the taillight of the car. Fortunately, the train was moving slowly, and the car was unoccupied when the accident occurred.

CSX No. 2617, a GP38-2, built in 1973 before the requirements for ditch lights, was retrofitted with them to meet the new FRA standard. Ditch lights improve safety at grade crossings and were required on all locomotives by Dec. 31, 1997.

6. Or at other times, to permit the passing of hand signals or the delivery of train orders or when the safety of an employee so requires."

For those that model the modern era, an additional lighting requirement was added in 1996. The Federal Railroad Administration (FRA) released a new requirement that locomotives traveling more than 20 mph and crossing through public highway grade crossings must have auxiliary lights (ditch lights), **7**. These auxiliary lights were required to be at least 36" above the rail head and at least 36" apart and form a triangle with the headlights, **8**. All railroads were required to have them installed by December 31, 1997. The ditch lights are required to be on when the headlight is set to "bright."

Many of the same requirements for extinguishing headlights apply to ditch lights and where the headlights are required to be dimmed, the ditch lights should be extinguished. This is to prevent blinding oncoming trains and crew members working in the area.

With the new surface-mounted LED lights available today, modelers can add ditch lights to older locomotives, or those that don't come factory-equipped with them. The ditch

9

Locomotive models, like this ScaleTrains.com GE C39-8, now come factory-equipped with ditch lights. The lights can be programmed to flash or remain on steady when the horn is activated based on the prototype practice.

lights can be programmed to flash with the horn, or can burn steady based on following your prototype railroads practices, **9**.

Blue signal display

"A blue signal or flag is used to signify that workmen are on, under, or between rolling equipment. When so displayed:

1. The equipment must not be coupled to;

2. The equipment must not be moved;

3. Other rolling equipment must not be placed on the track so as to reduce or block the view of a blue signal;

4. Rolling equipment must not pass a blue signal.

Blue signals must be removed only by the same craft or group that applied them."

While originally used by the railroads in their facilities and tracks, **10**, private industries also use blue signal protection to indicate a car that is not to be moved or coupled to as it

10 Blue signals (flags) are used to signify and protect workers on, under, or between rolling equipment and must not be moved. The blue signals must be removed only by the same craft or group that displayed them. In the above photo, the blue signals are displayed to prevent crews from moving or coupling to the locomotives until the blue signals are removed. *Joe Atkinson*

11 Industries also use blue signals to protect railcars that are connected to unloading hoses or workers that are in, under, or around the cars. These blue signals can only be removed by the facility that applied them and not the train crew. The tank car facility in the photo also has derails in addition to the blue signals indicating "Stop tank car connected" on each siding.

12 The End-of-Train Device (ETD) has replaced the traditional caboose on the end of almost all freight trains. The device sends a signal to a display in the cab of the locomotive indicating several parameters including train line air pressure. Although the devices come in different colors and shapes they all perform the same job. *Photo on left by Keith Armes*

is being loaded or unloaded. This also includes tank cars and covered hoppers with hoses attached, **11**. Railroad crews must have someone from the industry or facility remove the blue signal indication prior to entering the siding. These procedures keep workers safe and prevent damaging equipment if a car is moved.

Train crews are also required to visually inspect cars being pulled from an industry to ensure that hoses and loading/unloading plates are removed, hatches and outlets are secured, and industry employees are clear. The removal of the blue signal by the

industry does not eliminate the train crew's responsibility to perform this inspection.

End-of-Train devices

In the modern era where having a caboose on the end of a train is a rare occurrence, railroads now require either an End-of-Train Device (ETD) or a red flag be displayed on the rear of the last car. "When a train is occupying a main track during the period from one hour before sunset until one hour after sunrise and any other time that weather conditions restrict visibility to one-half mile or less, an illuminated

red light or orange amber marker light must be displayed on the rear of the last car to identify the rear end of the train, **12**. During all other times, a red flag, non-illuminated ETD, or marker light must be displayed on the rear of the last car to identify the rear of the train."

In addition, railroads operating in heavy grade territory must have an operating ETD with an emergency brake application feature regardless of time or visibility conditions. There are numerous other regulations that pertain to when an operating ETD is required. Modelers can refer to the rule

The Blue Ridge Scenic Railway (BRSR) has designated the track in front of the depot in Blue Ridge, Ga., as being within yard limits to allow crews to move under a controlled speed. This allows crews to move in any direction within yard limits without having to contact the dispatcher.

Large yards, such as this Norfolk Southern yard in Georgia, are under yard limits requiring crews to operate under a controlled speed. A controlled speed is one that will permit stopping within one-half the range of vision distance to an object of obstruction, not exceeding 10 mph. *Keith Armes*

13

book to determine if those conditions apply to their model railroad.

Modelers can easily replicate this requirement for an End-of-Train Device with simple scratchbuilt red flag detail, a non-operating ETD, or plan to use a car with an operating flashing ETD mounted to the coupler of the last car.

Movement of trains

The movement of trains is supervised by a control station or dispatcher, which will issue instructions as required. Each railroad will have specific rules that pertain to the movement of trains. The different types of train control can range from Timetable and Train Orders, Track Warrants, Centralized Traffic Control (CTC), Automatic Block Signaling (ABS), Verbal Block System (VBS), to a combination of systems. Crews must have a thorough understanding of the rules that pertain to each type of system.

On a small switching layout a VBS Absolute Block, Track Warrant, or Timetable and Train Order specifying the movement is all that is normally needed to operate prototypically in dark (unsignaled) territory. If the switching area is designated within yard limits, **13**, trains move at a Controlled Speed (or Restricted

The conductor, located on the same side of the locomotive as the engineer, directs the movement to a coupling using hand signals. Even in the modern era, many crews prefer to use hand signals when switching.

Speed), but not exceeding 10 mph. A controlled speed is one that will permit stopping within one-half the range of vision distance to an object or obstruction. Within yard limits, VBS rules do not apply and all trains operate under a controlled speed, which simplifies directing train movements and places responsibility for safe operation on the train crews.

Numerous books have been written on the subject of adapting prototype railroad train movement systems to a model railroad. Tony Koester's *Realistic Model Railroad Operation*, and the Operations Special Interest Group (OPSIG) publication, *A Compendium*

Prior to coupling to or moving a car, train crews must assure that all gang planks, spouts, conveyors, and hose connections are removed and cleared. The gang plank in this photo will need to be removed and the doors secured prior to movement by the train crew.

of Model Railroad Operations are excellent resources that modelers can use to gain a better understanding of each type of system and help you select the one that best fits your layout needs.

Flag protection

Flag protection is a procedure where a crew member is assigned to provide a warning to other trains that a train is stopped and fouling the main line. The Georgia Northeastern Railroad Operating Rules book states,

"When a train stops on a main track, the flagman, provided with flagging signals, must go back at the distance prescribed by special

16

The train crew in this photo performs a safety stop one car length prior to coupling to the other car. This allows the conductor to dismount and observe the coupling from a safe position on the ground. On the prototype it is not always sunny and 72 degrees, so operating safely is paramount in harsh weather conditions. *Joe Atkinson*

Above left: The switch points on this turnout have been painted white to improve visibility and permit crews to verify they are correctly aligned.

Above right: A conductor lines the switch for the proper route. As he operates the switch, he assures the points fit properly against the stock rail. In the modern era, more ergonomically designed switch throw levers, such as this bow handle design, were installed to reduce back injuries.

17

18

The normal position for a derail is in the derailing position. Most derails are painted a high visibility color, orange or yellow, to make them easily identifiable to train crews.

19

A crosstie is painted yellow to identify the clearance point for the siding. As long as cars are behind the yellow tie, the crew knows they will be in the clear of any cars or locomotives on the main line track.

instructions for the territory and display a lighted fusee. If no following train is seen or heard, the flagman must return half the distance to the rear of his train where he will remain, until he has either stopped a following train or is recalled.

"When rules require protection for the front of the train, a crew member with flagging signals must go forward immediately at least the distance prescribed by special instructions, display one lighted fusee, and remain at that location until recalled."

When a train inadvertently fouls the main track, protection must be provided against trains on that track in both directions.

Following these procedures is especially critical for prototype railroads in dark (un-signaled) territory. These flagging procedures protect a

stopped train from other trains that are operating on the line, thus preventing collisions. In the next chapter we will discuss ways model railroad crews can provide the same protection for their trains.

Switching procedures

Railroads have numerous rules that pertain to switching procedures. Many of these rules can easily be applied during model railroad operating sessions. Following are a few rules that govern all train crews when switching;

1. Make couplings at a speed of not more than 4 mph, **14**.

2. When coupling or shoving cars, take precautions to prevent damage or fouling other tracks, and when necessary, stretch the slack to ensure that cars are coupled.

3. Before placing cars in a track, ascertain that there is sufficient room in the track to hold the cars.

4. Before coupling to or moving cars that are being loaded or unloaded, notify persons in, on, or around the cars. Gang planks, spouts, conveyors, hose connections, and similar devices must be removed and cleared before the cars are coupled to or moved, **15**.

5. When feasible, cars must not be uncoupled on curves or in turnouts, but instead, the cars must be left on straight track to permit safe coupling to them.

6. When necessary to couple to cars on curves or in switches, ascertain that the couplers match.

7. When an engine is coupled to a train, the slack must be stretched to ensure that the coupling is made.

Numerous railroads require a "Safety Stop" one car length away from the car being coupled to, **16**. This procedure allows for the employee to verify the handbrake on the car is set and it is safe to couple to the car after performing an inspection. It also allows the employee to dismount, as most railroads do not allow the employee to ride to the coupling. Many railroads prohibit employees from mounting or

Above left: Any train crew member who enters a fouling position between the cars, such as to connect the air hoses between these two cars, must request "red zone" or "three step" protection. This is done to protect the crew member by preventing the train from moving while in this very dangerous fouling position.

Above right: After requesting and receiving "red zone" protection from the engineer, the conductor steps between the locomotive and the car to release the handbrake.

20

21

A train crew member "walks the train" checking the brakes and the cars for any defects. During an Initial Terminal Inspection and Test, the conductor will verify that the brakes apply and release on each car in the train.
Keith Armes

22

Using a brake stick, the conductor sets the handbrake on the covered hopper car. When using the brake stick, the conductor remains in a safe location outside of the fouling position between the cars. While some railroads encourage the use of brake sticks, others prohibit their use due to safety concerns. It all depends on the specific railroads policies and procedures. *Keith Armes*

dismounting moving equipment, while others allow it under certain conditions and speeds.

Some roads require a safety stop two car lengths before the end of a stub ended track and before shoving to a spot. This procedure avoids shoving cars off the end of a track as the movement is controlled. By following some of the same rules on our model railroads we can prevent accidents just like they do on the prototype.

Switches and derails

Rules on switches and derails are an important point of emphasis for the railroads, as not following the rules can lead to devastating consequences. Railroads require a job briefing be conducted before lining a hand-operated switch, crossover, or derail. The briefing will cover the means of communicating between the crew and how point protection will be provided.

Below are a few of the most important rules that apply to switches and derails;

1. The normal position for hand-operated switches on a main line track is for straight away movement, and the switch shall be lined and locked in that position when not in use.

2. Before a train or crew leaves a location where any hand-operated main line switch was operated, all crew members shall have a verbal communication to confirm the position of the switch.

3. Both switches of a crossover must be properly lined for the crossover before a train starts to make a crossover movement. The movement must be completed before either switch is restored to normal position, except when one crew is using both tracks connected by the crossover during continuous switching operations.

4. Employees lining switches must ascertain that the route is lined for the movement and the switch points fit properly, **17**.

5. Derails will be kept in the normal (derailing) position, whether or not there are cars on the track they protect, **18**.

6. Crews performing work at industries equipped with gates, doors, or movable bridges will not remove the derail until the gates, doors or movable bridges are fully opened. Movement must not be made until it is known that the gates or doors are fully opened and secured, that the removable bridge is properly lined and secured, and the derail is removed.

Rolling stock shall not be left where it will foul a connecting track.

1. On tracks where clearance point is indicated, leave equipment beyond the clearance point.

2. On tracks equipped with a derail; leave equipment beyond the derail.

If a clearance point is not indicated or visible, determine the clearance

23

After setting the handbrakes and performing a securement test, the conductor makes the cut and the locomotive pulls ahead. The conductor will look away as the air hoses separate to protect his eyes.
Joe Atkinson

24

All cars and locomotives on your layout should have the wheel gauge checked with an NMRA Standards gauge to assure reliable operations. Time spent on this inspection will contribute to a smooth-running operating session.

25

Operating locomotives with long heavy trains and many cars requires great skill from prototype engineers. Keeping the speed under control is one of the keys to safe train handling. *Keith Armes*

Above left: The conductor rides the side of the covered hopper car, providing point protection for the shove movement. By riding the car, it saves him from walking and reduces fatigue while safely performing the task of providing point protection.

Above right: Backing movements on a locomotive also require point protection in some cases. In this situation, a conductor is providing point protection for a reverse movement across a grade crossing in Miami, Fla. The buildings on each side reduce visibility when approaching the grade crossing and the engineer's vision is also reduced when operating in reverse on this GP40-2, so point protection is warranted.

26

point by standing outside of the rail of adjacent track and extending arm toward the equipment. When unable to touch equipment it will be considered clear.

In the modern era, railroads have mandated marking the clearance point on sidings indicating the point that cars must be behind to provide sufficient clearance for trains on the main line. This requirement can be met by painting a crosstie a specified color, making the clearance point easily identifiable to crews, **19**.

In addition to the rules above, some modern-era railroads require the conductor to state that they lined a switch and/or derail, the engineer request a double check, and the conductor state they double checked the switch and/or derail. This procedure stresses the importance of checking the status of a switch or derail and that it is properly lined to prevent accidents.

One of the most common problems that occur during an operating session is a crew running over a turnout thrown against them. By following the above rules and procedures, it will help prevent mishaps and keep your operating sessions running smoothly.

Three-step or red zone

One of the most dangerous jobs on the railroad is going between cars to hook up the air hoses. When crew members place themselves in a fouling position, special steps must be taken to insure the train is not going to move. A fouling position is defined as "when an employee and/or equipment is positioned in such proximity to a track that employees and/or equipment would be struck by moving equipment or train, or in any case within 4 feet of the field side of the near running rail," **20**.

Any employee working with an engine and crew will be required to communicate clearly to the engineer that they will be placing themselves in a fouling position prior to getting on or between equipment. This communication by radio will include the locomotive initial and number and any term indicating the person needs to foul the equipment.

The most common terms used to indicate they are in a fouling position are "requesting red zone" or "requesting three-step protection." The engineer will fully apply the independent brake, center the reverser, and open the generator field switch. The engineer

will then communicate to the person requesting to enter the fouling position the locomotive initial and number and then "centered and set" or "three step," at which time the person requesting permission may foul the equipment. The engineer may not alter the position of the independent brake, reverser, or field generator switch until further instructions have been received from the employee in the fouling position that they are in the clear.

Modelers can replicate these procedures by pausing when making a coupling and simulating the time it takes to enter the fouling position to hook up the air hoses. If working with a two-person switch crew, they can utilize the prototypical communication procedures of requesting permission to enter a fouling position, receiving a response from the engineer, and then clearing the fouling position.

Brake tests and car inspections

While our rolling stock does not have working brakes (yet), modelers can still replicate a brake test and car inspections during an operating session. On the prototype when trains

A conductor rides the platform of an open hopper car for a shove movement across a grade crossing. Selecting a car with a safe and comfortable riding position for the crew member to provide point protection is advised for long shove moves.

On railroads that frequently have long shove moves, a shoving platform is used. Old cabooses can be converted into shoving platforms by plating over the windows and proving safety appliances, which allow for a safer riding position for the conductor. *Keith Armes*

are assembled in yards, or cars are picked up or set out during switching operations, brake tests are performed, **21**. The two most common tests are the initial terminal test and the brake pipe leakage test. Knowing the exact procedures for each prototype test is not required for modelers to replicate performing the time it takes to complete the test.

Before departing a yard, model railroaders can "walk their train" as they simulate checking the brakes on each car. This time can also be used to verify the cars in the consist are properly blocked and correct for their train. During switching operations a brief pause can be done to simulate checking the brakes after a car is added to the consist.

When crews set cars out at an industry, or leave a cut of cars on a siding or main line, a "sufficient number of hand brakes" must be set to prevent the cars from moving, **22**. Railroads specify the number of hand brakes that are required to be set at each siding depending on conditions and the grade. Once the hand brakes are set, a "securement test" must be performed to assure the car does not move. On the prototype, the engineer creates slack in the coupler while it is still coupled and waits one minute to assure the hand brakes are holding. Once the test is completed, the

conductor will make the cut and the locomotive will pull ahead, **23**. Since our model train rolling stock does not have hand brakes that can be applied, operators should take a few seconds to replicate a securement test and make sure a car spotted at an industry does not roll. If it does, a "wheel chock" can be applied to hold the car in position.

Train crews on the prototype are required to inspect each car before coupling to it at an industry. This inspection looks for defects such as doors that don't close properly and any damage that causes a car to be unsafe. If any of these conditions are found, the crew will notify the dispatcher, who will contact the car repair department to have it repaired before it can be moved.

In addition, the crew will assure all dock boards, transfer plates, hose connections and similar connections have been removed and are in the clear, as well as all persons in or about cars have been warned and asked to vacate before the cars are switched.

Crews must not pull or switch covered or open top hopper cars with doors open. Top hatches and bottom outlets are required to be closed by the customer prior to pulling the car. Model railroaders can perform a similar inspection to check that a car is ready for pickup. Occasionally, a car could be identified as "defective," or not

ready to be moved, and crews would have to leave the car at the industry.

Train handling

"Good train handling is dependent upon two major factors:

"1. The judgment and skill of the engineer: To properly control a train, the engineer must anticipate and plan his actions and no matter what problem arises, it is his prompt assessment and reaction to the problem that can ensure smooth and proper train handling rather than damage to equipment or lading, a break-in-two, or worse, a derailment.

"2. The condition of the locomotive and car braking and mechanical system."

The above is quoted from the Georgia Northeastern Railroad Operating Rule Book, but it also pertains to the operation of our model trains. It is the skill of the model train engineer that determines the success of an operating session. In addition, if the locomotives and rolling stock are not up to NMRA mechanical standards, the operating session will suffer. All locomotives and rolling stock should be thoroughly checked and tested to meet the NMRA standards before being placed on the layout, **24**.

Slack action is a major force that train crews must deal with on the prototype. Slack action is created when

Above left: The location of hazardous materials in a train is determined by the hazard and what cars it is placed next to. This tank car, placarded for flammable liquids, is placed at the rear of the train.

Above right: This flat car, placarded for radioactive materials, requires special handling (note the Do Not Hump stencil) and placement in a train. *Keith Armes*

29

30

A buffer car is used on loaded bulk commodity trains containing hazardous materials to provide protection to the locomotive crew in the event of an accident. Many railroads have specifically designated buffer cars in service like the one in the photo. The BNSF car is stenciled for "Buffer Service Only, Do Not Load." *Keith Armes*

one portion of a train moves faster or slower relative to other portions of the train. Slack action can cause serious damage and/or a break-apart. To reduce slack action, trains must be started and stopped slowly. These same actions should be performed by model railroad engineers.

It is well known that the stopping ability of trains is affected by factors including speed, grade, and train weight, **25**. Engineers understand as speed increases more braking is needed to stop the train and the distance to stop is also increased. Model railroaders need to consider the same factors when controlling their trains and keep the speed reasonable for the job. Nothing

spoils the illusion of a model train replicating the actions of a prototype than one that is operated too fast on a layout.

One way prototype locomotive engineers can control their speed is with the use of dynamic brakes. Dynamic brakes use the energy of a moving train to generate electrical current at the traction motors, causing the motors to act as generators. The current is passed through a dynamic brake resistor grid, which creates electromagnetic force back pressure in the motors. The resistance of the motors then acts as a brake and slows the train. Some model locomotives with DCC now come equipped with a

dynamic brake feature that can be used in much the same way as the prototype to help slow the train when activated.

Shove move procedures

A shove move is one where the locomotive is to the rear of a cut of cars that are being moved in the direction away from the locomotive. When cars or engines are shoved, a member of the crew must be in a position to provide point protection by:

"1. Visually observing leading end of the movement to the location that the movement will be stopped.

"2. Being on equipment to observe leading end of the movement in the direction of movement, **26**.

Model railroaders can follow the same hazardous materials placement requirements as the prototype during their ops sessions. Note the hazardous material tank car placed between the two covered hopper cars. The refrigerated boxcar is not permitted to be next to the tank car, and placing the second covered hopper car behind the tank car allows for the locomotive to switch ends of the consist without changing the order of the cars.

"3. Being ahead of movement.

"Track will be considered clear and point protection not required:

"1. When a track has been pulled, and cars or engines are immediately shoved back into that track and has remained clear to location where movement will be stopped.

"2. When main track authority allows for movement in direction of shove, provided route is properly lined, road or pedestrian crossings will not be fouled and movement at restricted speed is not required.

"Rolling equipment shall not be shoved or pushed until the locomotive engineer participating in the move has been briefed by the employee who will direct the move. The job briefing shall include the means of communication to be used between the locomotive engineer and the employee directing the move and how point protection will be provided.

"During the shove or pushing movement, the employee directing the movement shall not engage in any task unrelated to the oversight of the shoving or pushing move."

When using a radio or hand signals to guide a shove move or other movement, the crew will use the number of car lengths to a stop or coupling. A car length is identified as a 50-foot distance for standardization of car counts. The crew member will indicate the distance in car lengths that they can see is clear and instruct the engineer to proceed. In half the distance specified, if the engineer does not hear from or see the crew member directing the movement, he shall stop the movement. Usually, when the count is down to five cars or less, the employee counts down car by car until he reaches half a car length, then 20 feet, 10 feet, 5 feet. Once the train has reached the end of the movement the crew member will state "that will do" over the radio, or give the proper hand signal, to indicate for the engineer to stop. The term "stop" on the radio is generally used for an emergency stop to prevent confusion.

Experienced prototype crews that know they will have a long shove move make plans to have a type of car on the point that is more comfortable for the employee to ride. It is much easier for the employee to stand on an end platform on a tank car, or other car type that has an end platform, than it is to ride the side of a car, 27. Note: Some railroads may have restrictions about employees riding a placarded hazardous materials tank car and prohibit it from being on the point of a shove move. Today, a few railroads still employ cabooses as "shoving platforms," which provides a secure location for the employee to ride and can be equipped with lights and a horn to sound at grade crossings, increasing the safety for the employee and the public, 28.

These same rules and procedures for shove moves can be adopted for a model railroad ops session. This type of operation works best when working with a two-person crew so that one person can observe the move while providing point protection and direct the engineer who is operating the throttle. The person providing point protection can count down or use hand signals to indicate the distance to a coupling or stop. This adds a very prototypical atmosphere to an ops session and keeps both crew members involved in the switching.

Hazardous materials car placement rules

Cars containing hazardous materials require special handling and placement in a train by the prototype railroads. Hazardous materials are classified according to their chemical and/or physical properties. Depending on how the hazardous material is classified

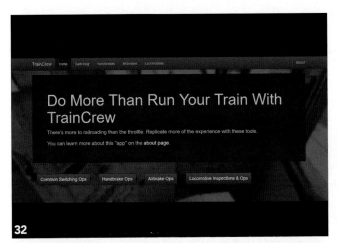

32

33

Ed Kapuscinski's Train Crew app allows model railroaders to duplicate the prototype procedures. The app has sections for Common Switching Ops, Handbrakes, Airbrakes, and Locomotive Inspections.

The Train Crew App can be downloaded onto your phone and used during operating sessions. By taking the time to follow the prototype operations it adds time to an ops session and gives you the experience of what a prototype train crew would be doing.

determines the rules for placement in a train, **29**. In addition, hazardous materials tank cars are identified as loaded or residue tank cars, which also affects the rules for their placement in a train.

Let's take a look at the rules for placement of a placarded hazardous materials car from the Norfolk Southern Railroad Hazardous Materials Position-in-Train Chart.

"When train length permits, a hazardous materials car must not be nearer than the sixth car from a locomotive or any occupied caboose, shoving platform, or passenger car. If length does not permit, it must be near the middle of the train.

"Must not be next to;

1. Open-top cars (including bulkhead flats) when any of the lading protrudes beyond the car ends or if shifted would protrude beyond the car ends.

2. Loaded flatcars except closed trailer on flat car/container on flat car equipment, multi-levels, and other specially equipped cars with tie-down devices for handling vehicles.

3. Railroad wheels loaded on wheel car flats, in gondolas with no ends, or loaded with the axles above the top of the cars.

4. Any rail cars, transport vehicles, or freight containers with temperature control equipment or internal combustion engine, when running or not.

5. Any placarded car in another placarding group, except it may be next to any residue placarded car.

"A locomotive, working or not working and regardless of placement in a train, is always considered as a locomotive for train placement of hazardous materials. A locomotive can NEVER be counted as a buffer car for train placement purposes. A buffer car is a non-placarded rail car. For a loaded bulk commodity train containing hazardous materials (ethanol, crude oil, etc.), a buffer car must weigh a minimum of 45 tons and be at least 41 feet long and not exceeding 70 feet in length," **30**.

As you can see from the rules, there is a great deal of information that the prototype train crews must take into account when determining the placement of cars in a train. How can we apply this information to our model railroads? Layout owners can establish their own simplified rules for placing a hazardous material car in a train. As an example, a loaded placarded hazardous materials tank car could require two buffer cars between it and a locomotive instead of the five required in the prototype rules and a residue tank car could require only one buffer car. Additional rules for placement next to mechanical refrigeration unit cars and flat cars could also be established for your model railroad, **31**, it is all up to you. Following these prototype car

placement rules adds another factor for the crews to consider when picking up and placing cars at an industry or building their train in a yard.

Train Crew App

Model railroader Ed Kapuscinski has developed a Train Crew app, **32**, that allows model railroaders to replicate many of the prototype procedures covered in this chapter. The app can be found at traincrew.conrail1285.com.

The app has tabs for Switching, Handbrakes, Airbrakes, and Locomotive Inspections. Each tab lists the various functions performed, has sound effects that are pertinent to the task, and a countdown clock. The time factor is generally set at a 4:1 fast clock so that the procedures do not take as long as they do on the prototype. Using the app while operating solo helps to slow down an ops session and allows you imitate how a prototype crew would go about doing the work, **33**.

By following the same prototype rules and procedures on our model railroads we can add time to an ops session by replicating the steps that a railroad uses to operate and safely switch cars. On small layouts it allows the layout to function like a much larger one by taking a few extra minutes to follow the prototype rules.

1

CHAPTER SIX

Detailing operations

Adopting prototype practices can enhance your operating session

The GNRR North Local arrives at Dow chemical on Tom's layout to switch the cars there. After opening the gate to the facility, the conductor will remove the derail and then line the turnout to the industry siding. The blue signal can only be removed by the person, group, or craft that applied it, so the crew will have to wait until it is removed by industry personnel (the layout owner) before coupling to the tank cars. In this case, the blue signal is used to protect tank cars from being moved that have hoses hooked up for unloading. Following the prototype procedures adds time to an ops session.

When modelers think about details, they usually imagine adding extra detail parts to locomotives, rolling stock, or structures, or incorporating scenery details that improve the look of our models. But details can also be operational and used to enrich an operating session by replicating those same situations and items that the prototype deals with on a daily basis. There are numerous operational details that can be added to your layout. Let's look at each one and explain how it can be integrated into your operating sessions to elevate them to a higher level of realism.

Above left: A blue signal has been applied and is locked in position to protect crews working on a train in Blue Ridge, Ga.

Above right: Blue signals have been applied to the tracks to prohibit movement or coupling to the locomotives stored at the Iowa Interstate Railroad's Council Bluffs enginehouse. In addition, blue signals have been hung on the side of locomotives 303 and 703, which indicates they are not to be started. *Joe Atkinson*

2

3

A forklift unloads a boxcar in Miami. A blue signal would specify the car is not to be moved or coupled to as it is being unloaded. Even after the blue signal is removed, train crews must be sure all ramps have been removed, and the boxcar doors are closed before coupling to the car.

4

A blue signal on a model railroad can be used to help slow down an ops session. Crews must request it be removed prior to coupling to the car or verify it has been removed prior to arrival when they switch the industry.

Enhancement to operations

By adding a few simple operational details to your layout, you can enhance your operations while following prototype practices, **1**. Some may consider these details as impediments to be disregarded as it slows down an ops session. On a small layout that is exactly what we want to do, slow down and replicate what the train crews do on the prototype. By integrating these details, it adds time and gives you more "play value" with a smaller layout.

As with most things in life,

you don't want to take things too far and have so many operational details it becomes overwhelming to the operators. Not every industry needs an operating detail, so choose the ones that make the most sense and incorporate them only at those locations.

Blue signals

As discussed in the previous chapter on prototype operations, a blue signal or flag is used to signify that workmen are on, under, or between

rolling equipment. When this signal is displayed, the rolling stock or locomotive must not be coupled to or moved until the blue signal is removed, **2**. The blue signal can only be removed by the person, group, or craft that applied it. Let's look at how a blue signal can be used on our layouts for operating sessions.

On cars that would have hoses connected to them to load or unload products, a blue signal would be used to protect personnel working around a car, and prevent damage if a car was

A piece of .020" wire was bent into the shape seen the photo for a blue signal. The U shape at the bottom clamps over the rail and the short leg holds it in the vertical position.

5

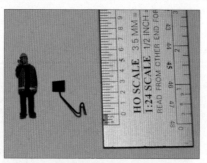

An HO scale figure is placed next to a blue signal to indicate its relative size. The rectangular blue sign is a scale 18 x 12 inch piece of aluminum flashing; .010" styrene could also be used for the sign.

6

Ring Engineering Inc. has an operating end-of-train device that can be added to any freight car. The modeler replaces the car's original truck with the ETD one with the electrical pickups. Next, you replace the car's original coupler with the one wired with the ETD. *Ring Engineering Inc.*

7

A removable ETD was built from styrene, wire, and a red jewel. While the ETD does not flash, it can be applied to any car on the layout.

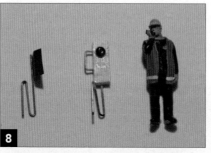

8

A 1" long piece of .015" music wire was bent into an "N" shape to hold the electronic ETD or the red flag to the coupler on a train car. The ETD was made from a small piece of styrene and the flag is a piece of red vinyl. While slightly oversized compared to the prototype, it makes them easier to remove and install during an operating session.

to be moved before the hoses were disconnected. In addition, blue signals can be used for cars positioned at a location where docks would be placed to access the cars with forklifts, **3**. One can only imagine the results if a boxcar was to be moved as a forklift was entering or exiting the car.

At these types of industries, it is appropriate to have a blue signal placed on the track to prevent moving a car before all precautions have been taken to make it safe to move. Modelers can place a blue signal on the track prior to an ops session, and have one member designated as the employee in charge of the facility, and only they can remove the blue signal when requested, **4**. This makes the operating crew slow down and verify the blue signal has been removed, and if not, they have to request it be removed before they can switch the industry.

Making a blue signal is an easy project that only requires a couple of

items. First, bend a piece of .020" wire into the shape you see in the photo **5**. It starts off with a small leg that runs parallel to the rail to help it stand up straight. Next, bend the wire up and over about the height of a piece of rail so that the flag actually "clamps" onto the rail to help hold it. Then bend the wire back up and at a slight angle. Bend the wire straight up for about the last scale 2 feet. The sign portion is a small piece of aluminum flashing cut to size. A piece of .010" styrene can also be used for the sign portion. The size of the sign is about 18 x 12 scale inches, although the exact size is not that critical. I used cyanoacrylate adhesive (CA) to attach the sign to the wire post, then the entire assembly was

painted blue, **5**. Decal companies offer blue signal "men working" signs that can be applied to the sign if desired, but many blue signals have no wording on them, so you can choose how you want to model them.

End-of-Train Device

Years ago it was easy to identify the end of a train, as it had a caboose. As railroads began to retire cabooses, they needed a way to identify the end of a train and the End-of-Train Device (ETD or EOT) was developed.

These devices can range from a simple red flag inserted the rear coupler of the last car on the train, or can be an electronic ETD that sends a radio signal to a receiver in the cab of the locomotive indicating train line air pressure and other parameters. The electronic ETD also has a flashing light that improves visibility at night and inclement weather. Railroads have rules as to which type of ETD can be used, and when it is required as discussed in the previous chapter.

Ring Engineering Inc. offers an HO scale flashing ETD that can be installed on your own car, **6**. These ETDs pick up power from truck-mounted bushings on the axles of the car. The track power then operates a flashing red light on the ETD.

The ETD comes in a variety of prototypical colors, two different wheel sizes, and standard or long wire lengths for the device. The flashing red light is a very nice detail and accurately captures the look of the prototype ETD.

Another option is to make your own non-operating electronic ETD. While it won't have a flashing red light, it can be moved to any car to identify the end of the train, **7**.

The design for my ETD came from Jim Talbott, who models the Wheeling & Lake Erie in the modern era. Jim was looking for an easy way to identify the last car of his trains during an operating session with an ETD that could be inserted on any cars' coupler. Jim's friend Doug Tagsold designed an ETD for him based on an original design by Bruce Carpenter. Doug modified Bruce's design by adding a piece of wire so the ETD could be placed over the knuckle of a coupler. I received one of Doug's ETD's from Jim and used it as a prototype to build my own.

To make your own HO scale ETD, begin with a piece of .080" x .100" styrene cut ⁵⁄₁₆" long. Drill a no. 76 hole in the bottom of the styrene for the mounting wire and two holes on the side for a handle.

Next, bend a 1" long piece of .015" music wire into an "N" shape with the last leg of the N slightly extended above the other side. The left and center leg of the "N" are approximately ¼" long, with the remaining leg being about ½" long.

Insert the wire into the bottom of the styrene and glue it in place. Bend another piece of wire to form a handle and insert it in the holes drilled on the side.

Next, paint the ETD the color of your choice or follow your prototype's color practices for the device. End-of-Train devices can be painted many colors with yellow, orange, or gray being the most common. I found a small red ruby lens that worked perfectly for the red light in a scrapbooking materials section of a local store. The ruby was glued in place on the ETD. Now you have a portable ETD that you can install on the last car of your train. The ETD is slightly oversized, but that makes it easier to install and remove during an ops session, **8**.

9 A red flag marks the end of a train on Tom's layout. The crew will remove the flag when it switches the car and install it on the last car before departure.

10 A flag man with a red lantern is positioned on the track to provide protection for the rear of the stopped train on Tony Koester's layout. The flagman picks up power from the rails to illuminate the lantern. The flagging distance was shortened for the photograph. The Logic Rail Technologies mobile fusee pro could also be used in a similar manner. *Tony Koester*

11 This flip-over style derail protects the main line from a runaway car on a siding by derailing the car away from the main. The derail works by lifting the wheel off the rail and purposely derailing the car to stop its movement.

A split-point derail works similar to a turnout except it derails a car instead of diverting it to another route. The normal position for this derail is for the diverging route, which functions to derail the car. The switch stand signal for this derail is missing, which makes it harder for crews to see it is in the derailing position. *Scott Chatfield*

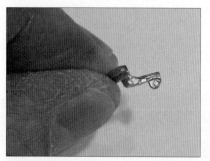

The derail casting is the main piece needed from the Alexander Scale Models Hayes Derail set for the operating derail project. Drill a number 70 hole in the main body of the derail casting at the correct location for a hinge pin.

Cut off the leg portion of the derail casting just past the main body where you drilled the hinge pin hole.

Insure the derail lays flat in the removed position so locomotives and rolling stock can pass over it. Once you are satisfied with the position, glue it in place while the derail is resting on the rail.

The easiest of all ETDs to model is a red flag. Many railroads still use a flag during daylight hours on their local trains. To make a red flag ETD begin with bending a 1" long piece of .015" music wire into an "N" shape the same as you did for the non-operating ETD. For the flag portion, I used a small piece of red vinyl from a survey marking flag. Cut a piece of vinyl to a scale 18 inch square for the flag. The flag was glued to the wire with CA after assuring the flag pointed to the rear when installed on the coupler, **9**.

Now with either the flag or non-operating ETD, crews on my model railroad simulate walking the train prior to departure and insert an ETD in the last coupler to indicate the brake test was performed and the train is ready to depart. During switching moves the ETD is removed and placed in a visible area on layout, then reinstalled once the switching is completed.

Flag protection

As mentioned in the chapter on prototype operations, crews are required to provide flag protection to prevent collisions with a train that is stopped on the main line. Model train crews must provide similar protection for their trains. This can be accomplished with a small crew figure with a red flag in their hand or a lighted fusee device, **10**.

Operating crews should have access to a train crew figure that would indicate approaching trains must stop prior to reaching a train stopped on a main line. The figure can be placed at a safe distance that will allow adequate stopping distance for approaching trains.

An electronic module designed to represent a lighted fusee can also be used as flagging protection. Logic Rail Technologies (logicrailtech.com) has developed the Fusee Pro/M, a mobile circuit board that has an adjustable time rate that replicates a burning fusee. The fusee device gets its power from the rails and illuminates a flickering red LED light, warning approaching crews to stop. Once the crew clears the main, or begins moving again, the fusee is removed.

Derails

A derail is a device used to prevent fouling or blocking a track by unattended rolling stock or unauthorized movements of trains. The device purposely derails the equipment as it rolls over it. While re-railing equipment is costly, it prevents greater damage, injury, or death if the equipment rolls past the derailing point and fouls the main.

There are a few different types of derails, with the most common being the wedge type, **11**. This style

Crews use a bamboo skewer to flip the derail over into the removed position. The derail lays flat so locomotives can pass over it. Once the derail is removed, the crew opens the gate and has the industry representative (the layout owner) remove the blue signal. After completing the switching operations, the crew closes the gate and reapplies the derail.

16

17

MagnaLock Brake Lines use small magnets on the ends of the flexible air hoses to connect them together.

18

As the cars approach each other, the magnetic ends of the hoses attract and the hoses connect together.

19

When the cars are uncoupled, the air hoses automatically separate as the car pulls away.

of derail has a wedge-shaped piece of steel that rests on top of the rail in the derailing position. If a car or locomotive attempts to pass over it, the derail lifts the wheel up and off the rail, directing it to the outside of the gauge and derailing the equipment. When the derail is removed, it moves or folds out of the way and the equipment can safely pass by.

Another type of derail, a split point derail, is similar to a standard turnout except the switch only has one point rail and the diverging route rail terminates within a few feet of the main line, **12**. These types of derails are less common, but still used on the prototype.

A portable derail can be used to temporarily protect equipment that is being worked in conjunction with a blue signal or flag protection.

The rules that apply to derails are;

• The normal position for derails is in the derailing position.

• All derails must be equipped with

a locking device and be locked when not in use.

• Derails will be kept in the normal derailing position whether or not there are cars on the track they protect.

Modelers can make operating derails that add a prototypical step that has to be performed before switching an industry protected by a derail.

An operating derail was made for my layout by modifying an Alexander Scale Models 120-9501 Hayes Derail set. The set was originally designed as a switch stand style derail, but I converted it to a flip over style.

To begin the project, drill a hole in the hinge point of the derail casting using a number 70 drill bit, **13**. After drilling the hole, cut off the arm portion of the casting, **14**.

Next, place the derail in position and locate the position for the hinge point. Remove any ballast from under the hinge point so it will not interfere with the casting as it rotates into the removed position. Cut two small .060"

square pieces of .040" styrene and glue them on top of each tie at the point where the hinge pin would rest. The styrene is used to elevate the hinge point so the derail is able to flip over and lay flat in the removed position.

Next, cut a piece of .020" music wire ¼" long for the hinge pin, and insert it into the derail casting. Check the assembly with everything in position and make any necessary adjustments to the casting to allow the derail to flip completely over, **15**.

Once you are satisfied with the operation of the derail, use CA to attach the hinge pin wire to the two styrene blocks, making sure not to get any glue in the hinge point of the casting. The derail should be placed on top of the rail, in the derailing position, when the hinge pin is glued in place.

When crews operate on my layout, they are required to remove the derail before lining the switch and confirm the derail is removed, **16**. Yes, if they forget to remove it, and run over

Automatic grade crossing signals add action and a prototypical detail to a layout, but they also add additional operational details. As trains approach a grade crossing, the locomotive should sound its whistle or horn in the appropriate sequence. In addition, grade crossings should not be blocked for extended periods of time during switching moves. Crews should also avoid unnecessarily activating the grade-crossing circuit.

the derail, they function exactly as those on the prototype and derail the equipment. Once crews have finished their switching duties, they reapply the derail and confirm its position before departing.

Magnetic air hoses

Connecting air hoses between cars is a very dangerous and time-consuming job on the prototype. Railroad crews must request "red zone" or "three step protection" to enter a fouling position to connect the air hoses. Once the hoses are connected, the angle cocks are opened and allow air to flow through the hoses between the cars for the train braking system.

While our model trains don't need to connect the air hoses between the cars for braking, this procedure can now be replicated thanks to North American Railcar Corporation's (NARC) MagnaLock Brake Lines sold through Pacific Western Rail Systems (PWRS). The company has developed flexible rubber air hoses that use magnets on the end of each hose to connect the air hose from each car together, **17**. The magnetic air hoses can replace any standard plastic

air hose or be installed on cars that previously had no air hoses.

The MagnaLock Brake Line conversion starter kit includes everything a modeler needs to install magnetic air hoses on 10 cars or locomotives. The kit also includes a gluing jig to aid the modeler with installation. The air hoses are compatible with all brands of couplers.

Once the air hoses are installed on the cars, the crew can then include procedures to confirm they are connected during switching operations. The MagnaLock brake lines work automatically. As the cars are pushed together, the magnets attract each other and then connect, **18**. Crew members can then "walk the train" to confirm all hoses are connected. Once a crew sets out a car, the air hoses automatically disconnect as the train pulls away from the car, just like they do on the prototype, **19**. The MagnaLock brake lines add another prototypical procedure that can be included in an operating session. While they may not be practical for a large layout with many cars, they are perfect for a small switching layout.

Grade crossings

Lights flash, bells ring, and the gates come down, all signifying that a train is approaching a grade crossing. An operating grade crossing signal on our layouts adds a lot of visual impact and action to capture the viewers' attention, **20**. Grade crossing signals are a great operational detail, but there is more to it that just the operating crossing signal, there are the prototype rules and procedures that must be followed that involve grade crossings.

As discussed in the chapter on prototype operations, the locomotive must use the proper horn signal and ring the bell when approaching a public grade crossing. There are a few exceptions to this rule in communities that have enacted "quiet zones," but for our purposes we will consider all grade crossings as requiring signaling. With sound-equipped decoders becoming common in most models, crews should be encouraged to use the bell and horn when approaching a grade crossing.

A few other rules that pertain to grade crossings are as follows;
• Trains or cars must not stand on crossings more than a reasonable time without being uncoupled, to

21

If a grade crossing is going to be blocked by a train, the crew should split the train so the crossing can be used by motorists. The rail cars should be left no closer than one car length away from the crossing for safety reasons. In this photo, the crew has split the train at the grade crossing while performing its switching duties down the line.

22

An operating overhead door adds a prototypical step for the switch crews when they swap out cars at the Georgia Metal Coaters facility. The door is manually operated by turning a rooftop ventilator to open and close the door. Here the crew waits until the door is fully opened to switch the cars inside.

permit safe passage of pedestrians and vehicular traffic.

• Municipal ordinances must be obeyed.

• Every reasonable effort must be made to avoid unnecessary operation of the automatic grade-crossing warning devices.

• Cars or other equipment must not be left standing within the insulated joints at grade crossings so equipped.

• When practicable, cars or other equipment must not stand or be left either within 100 feet of crossing equipped with automatic grade-crossing warning devices or within 200 feet of crossings not so equipped.

These same rules can be incorporated into our operating sessions while making a few modifications to accommodate our shorter distances and compressed time factors.

On my layout, I have established a one-car-length rule for leaving cars near a grade crossing, **21**. While this is a little closer than the prototype allows, it is easy for crews to remember and implement.

For those who use a fast clock, a 10 minute time limit for blocking a grade crossing is a reasonable compromise for a model railroad operating session. Crews should also strive not to unnecessarily activate the grade crossing circuit.

By following these prototype rules

it adds time to an ops session as crews have to consider not blocking a grade crossing or making provisions for splitting their train at the crossing if they are going to be blocking it for an extended period of time.

Overhead doors

An operating overhead rolling door is an interesting detail that can be added to your layout. I modeled an operating overhead rolling door on my layout based on a prototype facility served by the Georgia Northeastern Railroad, **22**.

I began by determining the height of the overhead door by measuring the tallest piece of rolling stock I owned and added a few scale feet for extra clearance. This measurement was rounded off to 2½" for the height of the door.

I needed the structure to be tall enough that the door would be able to slide up completely and the bottom would clear the top of the door opening in the fully raised position. In addition, I needed extra height above the door for the gear mechanism to engage the gear rack which would be mounted on the back of the door. To accomplish these requirements, the model structure is at least two and a half times the height of the door.

I located the center of the door opening on the structure to align with the center of the siding that would enter the facility. I cut the opening 2"

wide by 2½" high. Next I trimmed the exterior of the opening with Evergreen no. 292 .080" angle. I used Plastruct Bondene plastic solvent cement to glue the angle to the edge of the door opening. The finished doorway opening is a scale 14 feet wide by 18 feet high.

On the inside of the door opening I used Evergreen no. 156 .060" x .125" strip styrene to frame the opening. This step adds some structural rigidity and thickness to the wall opening which can be seen when the door is open.

To make the track that the overhead door would slide in, I used Plastruct no. 90541 H column. The web in the H column perfectly accommodates the thickness of the door, and allows it to side up and down without binding.

I glued one side of the H column to the inside edge of the opening, **23**, and allowed it to dry. Next, I cut an overhead door using Evergreen no. 4526 metal siding. This siding replicates the type of corrugated metal that is used in a prototypical overhead rolling door. I cut the door 2¹⁄₁₆" wide by 4⁵⁄₁₆" high with the corrugations going horizontally across the door.

The excess height of the door allows room to attach a gear rack and mount an operating mechanism above the top of the door opening. To glue the second H column in place I used the door as a guide to properly locate it. I held the door in position and then used a micro brush dipped in Plastruct

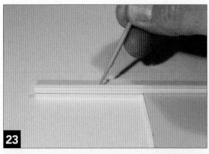

23

The H column is glued to the inside of the door opening to provide a track for the roll-up door.

24

Tom placed the overhead door in position, then aligned the other H column using the door as a guide. Next, he applied glue to the outside edge of the H column.

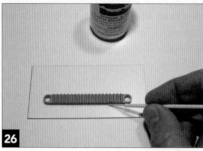

25

The Lego Technic gear reducer allows for flexibility in mounting it to the structure and provides a smooth gear-driven operation for the door.

26

The gear rack was positioned on the back of the door so it would engage the center of the gear reducer. With the rack location marked, the door was removed, making it easier to glue the rack perfectly vertical on the door.

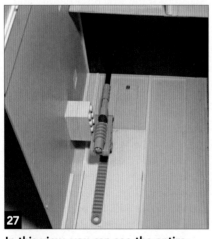

27

In this view, you can see the entire assembly. The operating shaft was extended through the roof using an additional Lego axle and coupler.

28

To open the door, a train crew member turns the operating knob disguised as roof-top ventilator.

The key components to make the door operate are a gear reducer mechanism and a gear rack. I found a Lego Technic gear reducer set at an online auction site, **25**. The gear ratio is 1:24, which provides a very slow, smooth operation for the overhead door. The second component, the Lego gear rack, comes in various lengths. The gear rack must be at least the height of the door opening so the door will raise completely. I found one that had the gear portion 2½" long, which worked perfectly for my installation.

Additional components to attach the gear reducer to the structure and extend the drive axle can be found online, on the Lego website, and at various retailers.

To mount the gear reducer to the structure I used two standard Lego bricks glued together. I press fit the gear reducer to the bricks using the holes in the side frame of the reducer. This assembly located the gear reducer just off center of the door opening.

I held the gear assembly in position and located the proper height so the bottom of the gear reducer was just above the opening of the doorway and marked that location. Next, I placed the door in the opening and temporarily held the gear rack to the back of the door to determine the correct distance to mount the gear assembly where it would engage the gear rack. I marked the location and then glued the assembly to the side wall of the structure using Plastruct Plastic Weld cement, which is designed to bond dissimilar plastics such as styrene and ABS.

Once the glue dried for the gear assembly, it was time to determine the exact location of the gear rack on the back of the door. The gear rack was located so that the first tooth would engage the center of the round gear of the gear reducer. I marked the location of the gear rack and removed it from the structure to make it easier to glue. I glued it into position making sure the gear rack was perfectly vertical on the door, **26**.

With the gear rack and reducer mounted in the structure, it was time to extend the operating shaft to the

Bondene to glue the outside of the H column, **24**.

I was very careful not to get any glue in the inside track or on the back of the door. I slid the door up as I glued the upper portion of the H column in place. Once the H column

was tacked in place, I removed the door by sliding it out the bottom and applied glue to the inside edge of the H column. While the glue dried, I lightly sanded the edges of the door, then once the glue dried, checked that the door would slide easily in the track.

Before lining the switch to the industry siding, the crew must open the gate. The gate is operated manually by turning a handle on the layout fascia. An operating gate adds one more realistic step for switch crews.

29

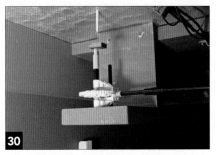

30

The Lego gear reducer is the key component that makes the gate operate. The mechanism operates smoothly, and slowly opens the gate when the operating handle is turned. A weight was added to the long leg of the fence gate before the wire was bent to help hold it in the slot on the gear reducer output shaft, and provide a counterbalance for the gate.

roof so that it could be operated by hand. I extended the operating shaft by using a coupling and another Lego axle piece to extend the shaft through the roof of the structure, **27**. I used a Walthers roof type ventilator left over from another structure to act as a knob on the end of the shaft. The hole in the bottom of the ventilator was slightly larger than the diameter of the shaft so I used Evergreen no. 142 .040" square strip to fill in the gap between the shaft and the ventilator. I used CA to attach the shaft to the ventilator. Once the glue was dry, I determine the correct length and cut the shaft so that it would sit flush on the roof of the structure with the other end attached

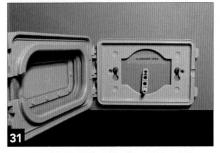

31

A hinged electrical outlet cover was used to protect the operating handle of the gate. The handle is made from Lego Technic pieces.

to the gear reducer shaft coupler.

When the local crew arrives at the facility, the door is closed and must be opened to access the cars needing to be switched. To open the door, the operator turns the roof top ventilator counter-clockwise until the door reaches the fully open position, **28**. This action takes approximately 30 seconds for the door to fully open. The crew then switches the cars for the facility, then closes the door by rotating the ventilator clockwise once the switching is completed. This animated feature adds one more realistic step that the crew must perform when switching my layout and duplicates what the prototype crew encounters when they switch this facility.

Industry fence gates

With security being a high priority at all facilities, fence gates at industries are becoming more common. Railroads

32

Joe Atkinson added small luggage padlocks to the turnout control levers on his layout. The locks prohibit the use of the turnout until they are unlocked and removed from the eye hook on the lever. *Joe Atkinson*

33

Once the lock is removed from the eye hook on the control lever, the switch can be lined. The opened lock is hung on the eye hook on the fascia. This simple operation adds a prototypical step to switching cars on Joe's layout. *Joe Atkinson*

typically use a railroad lock to secure the gate and the conductor uses his or her switch lock key to open the gate when it is time to switch the facility. The Georgia Northeastern requires

34

Those locks marked with a blue tag are only to be operated by the Mechanical Department (the layout owner) and crews must ask for permission to have the locks removed. This procedure follows the prototype blue signal procedures discussed earlier. *Joe Atkinson*

35

Joe Atkinson added the switch lock key to a key ring on the end of the uncoupling pick that the crews use to keep it handy and from getting misplaced. *Joe Atkinson*

36

Scott Thornton added G scale switch stands to small shelves on the fascia of his layout. The switch stands operate very prototypically and are connected to the turnouts with cable linkage. *Scott Thornton*

that any gate across a siding must be opened prior to lining the switch to the siding. I wanted to build an operating gate so my crews would have to go through the same steps as the prototype does to switch a facility with a fence gate, **29**.

I scratchbuilt my fence for the facility using .020" music wire and tulle for the fencing. Using the same techniques, I constructed the gate using .025" music wire to make the assembly more rigid. I did not extend the middle and end post below the bottom rail so the gate could swing freely over the track. I made the post on the hinge side of the gate 6" long and added diagonal supports to the gate frame. I attached the tulle with CA and then painted the assembly. Finally, I added EZ Line to the top of the posts to represent barbed wire.

Next, I inserted a 4" piece of ³⁄₃₂" styrene tubing through the foam base where the hinge side of the gate would be located. This tubing is used to adjust the height of the gate and provide a conduit for the shaft that operates the gate. I inserted the long leg of the gate through the tubing. It exited the bottom of the tube on the underside

of the layout. I adjusted the height of the gate using the styrene tube so the bottom of the gate would just clear the tracks when it opened and closed.

I looked for a simple mechanical way to operate the gate and discovered it in another Lego Technic set. The set had a gear reducer mechanism that has a worm gear driven by an input shaft. The mechanism takes a horizontal rotating action and converts it to a vertical rotating shaft that can rotate in either direction. While the Lego gear set that I used has been discontinued, I was able to locate a similar mechanism on an online auction site by searching Lego gear reducers. Additional connection pieces can be purchased online through various websites or directly from Lego.

A small shelf was built to hold the mechanism at the proper height and I located it to line up precisely under the long leg of the gate. I mounted the mechanism to the shelf, then extended the input shaft through the fascia and attached a crank handle to the end using other pieces from the Lego set. After drilling a hole in a small weight, I slipped it onto the long leg of the gate from below to act as a

counterweight for the gate. Next, I bent the long leg of the gate at a 90 degree angle and then 180 degrees back to create a upside down T at the proper height to connect it to the mechanism. I cut the excess wire off after I was satisfied with the location and height. I used a shaft connection bracket from the Lego set to extend the output shaft and connect it to the gate leg, **30**.

To prevent the crank handle from being bumped accidentally, I used a hinged exterior electrical outlet cover to protect the crank handle, **31**. Crews open the cover and access the gate control crank handle when they need to open the gate. The gate opens as you turn the crank handle clockwise. To close it, simply reverse the direction.

Above left: A conductor removes a wheel chock from a covered hopper car on a siding outside of a facility. The wheel chock is an extra precaution taken to prevent the cars from rolling if the handbrakes don't hold.

Above right: Depending on the specific railroad, wheel chocks may be applied to locomotives that are parked on a grade. Here, the Blue Ridge Scenic Railway has applied wheel chocks to the locomotive that is parked outside the depot in Blue Ridge, Ga.

37

This simple system operates smoothly and reliably, and adds a realistic step that crews have to perform as they switch the industry.

Switch locks

Joe Atkinson models the Iowa Interstate's Subdivision 4, the western-most 49 miles of the railroad from Atlantic to Council Bluffs, Iowa, in May 2005. He added switch locks to his layout to enrich his operating sessions.

"I've long been intrigued by the idea of adding working switch locks to the layout as Lance Mindheim, Trevor Marshall, James McNab, and others have done," Joe wrote. "They'd slow down operations a bit, draw my crews and me deeper into thinking like our prototype counterparts, and prevent crews from operating on trackage that's controlled by the Engineering (Maintenance-of-Way (MOW)) or Mechanical departments (diesel house/carmen) on the prototype. However, I'd never seen someone add locks to push/pull-style turnout controls in the fascia like mine, so I was unsure of how to proceed. During a trip to my local home improvement store to consider hardware options, I landed on the solution of using screw eyes and small padlocks.

"My turnout controls consist of

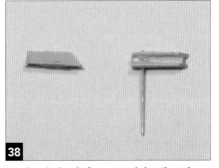

38

A wheel chock for a model railroad can be built using a piece of 3/32" styrene H column. The styrene was cut with a 45 degree angle on one end, and a piece of .015" wire was added for a handle. A small amount of poster tack was applied in the channel of the wheel chock that sits on top of the rail to help keep it from sliding.

wood dowels passing from a DPDT paddle switch under the layout and extending through the fascia. All are oriented so that they're pushed in when the turnout's lined for the through route and pulled out to line it for diverging. By attaching one screw eye to the dowel and another to the fascia such that the openings in them align with one another when the control is pushed in, I can pass a small luggage padlock through them, preventing the turnout from being moved without first unlocking and removing the padlock, **32** and **33**.

39

The wheel chock helps prevent a car from rolling and is easily removed when the car needs to be picked up.

"It's important to note that not all turnouts are locked. On my prototype, Transportation Dept. switch locks (those for which train crews have keys) are only used outside of yard limits, controlling only those turnouts that diverge from the main track. For the segment of the line I model on my layout, that means a total of only seven locks that crews typically deal with. There are also three blue-tagged Mechanical Dept. locks, **34**, restricting access to enginehouse and RIP track facilities, and three yellow-tagged Engineering Dept. locks for tracks that are used exclusively for the storage of MOW cars. Train crews must contact the appropriate department (the layout owner) to gain access to those areas.

"During formal operating sessions, I assign two-person crews, engineer

40

41

The conductor has deployed a fusee on Lance Mindheim's Miami Downtown Spur layout to help alert drivers that the un-signaled railroad grade crossing is being used by the local. This follows a similar procedures done by prototype crews to enhance safe operations at un-signaled grade crossings. *Lance Mindheim*

The circuit board for the fusee is available from Logic Rail Technologies. The board can be powered from AC or DC power. *Lance Mindheim*

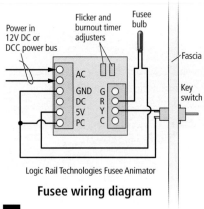

Fusee wiring diagram

42

The fusee wiring diagram indicates how to connect the circuit board to your layout electrical system and connect the accessories to the output functions. *Lance Mindheim*

and conductor, allowing each to focus strictly on the tasks associated with their job role. The addition of switch locks was seamless in that environment, and added even more interest to the conductor's role as they further emulate their prototype counterparts. Most of my operations, though, involve me running solo, and the primary concern I had when starting down this path was the need to have two hands free when locking and unlocking turnouts, while also juggling a ProtoThrottle, paperwork, and an uncoupling pick. As it turned out, that wasn't an issue at all. Adding a key ring for the switch lock key on

the blunt end of my uncoupling picks, **35**, meant I had nothing additional to carry, and with the ProtoThrottle on a lanyard around my neck, all I had to do to operate a lock was to either hang my paperwork clipboard on fascia hooks that were already in place, or to tuck it under one arm.

"Looking back, I wish I'd added switch locks long ago, as they provide a simple, inexpensive means of immersing operators further into the thinking of prototype crews. In addition to all the benefits mentioned above, the locks have been a great conversation-starter when non-hobbyists visit the layout, as they almost always ask about them. That's given me a great opportunity to explain prototype modeling to them, hopefully opening their eyes to interesting aspects of the hobby they hadn't considered previously."

Large scale switch stands

To add a prototypical feel to operating a turnout, Scott Thornton uses a Sunset Valley Railroad G scale switch stand to move the points on his turnouts. Scott mounted the switch stand to a shelf on the fascia and connected the switch stand mechanism to the turnout throw lever with a cable linkage. Crews operate the switch just as the prototype crews do and it requires them to walk into position near the turnout rather than flipping a toggle switch from a control panel, **36**.

Railcar Chocks

Occasionally railcar wheel chocks need to be applied to prevent a car from moving when the brakes are being worked on, or industry rules and track conditions require them to be applied. A railcar chock is a wedge shaped device that is installed on top of the railhead and the wedge portion goes up against the wheel. This additional safety device prevents a car from rolling in addition to the hand brakes being applied, **37**.

Many times on our layouts there is a siding on a slight grade, which causes problems when we set out a car as it wants to roll away. Since our model rolling stock does not have working brakes, a railcar wheel chock is a good option to keep the car in place.

I built a simple railcar chock from a ⅜" long piece of Plastruct (no. 90542) ³⁄₃₂"/2.4 mm styrene H column. I cut a 45 degree angle on one end so that when the H column was placed on the railhead it would angle toward the bottom of the wheel. I also designed a wheel chock with a small handle, made with .015" music wire, to aid in installing the wheel chock just like some of the ones on the prototype have, **38**. Most prototype railcar wheel chocks I saw were painted yellow or orange for high visibility, so I painted mine yellow. After the paint was dry I placed a small amount of reusable poster putty in the bottom of the H channel. This removable non-toxic,

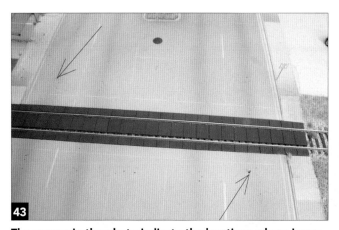

43

The arrows in the photo indicate the locations where Lance drilled holes for the fusee lights and installed them. *Lance Mindheim*

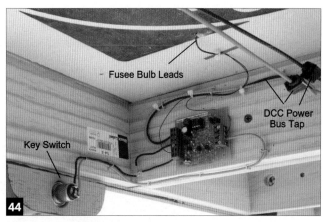

44

In this view of the final installation of the fusee circuit board, you can see how the circuit board is wired to the layout and the key switch. The fusee circuit is easy to install and adds another realistic feature to a switching operation. *Lance Mindheim*

45

Scott Thornton wanted to be able to have a "movable riding conductor" on his layout. He added small magnets to the sides of his freight cars so a conductor figure could be attached to the side of the car. *Scott Thornton*

non-staining adhesive will hold the wheel chock in position and allow it to easily be removed when necessary. This simple operational detail works just like the ones on the prototype and solves a problem that many model railroaders encounter on their layouts, **39**.

Fusee

Lance Mindheim wrote an article in the January 2010 issue of *Model Railroader* magazine about using a modeled fusee (aka flares) to protect an un-signaled grade crossing during switching operations, **40**. On the prototype, fusees are used by switch crews to warn motorists that the train

crew is operating in the area and to be alert for a flagman. This is an excellent operational detail to add to your layout that mimics a prototype procedure.

Lance wrote in his article; "A quick search on the net found that Logic Rail Technologies (logicrailtech.com) produces a circuit board to represent fusees, **41**. Their fusee product is available in two sizes, the smaller size being appropriate for HO scale. The board can be powered from a standard 12-16 volt DC power supply or your DCC power bus. If you tap into your DCC power bus for power, make sure you use the AC terminals on the Logic Rail board, **42**.

"The simple circuit board comes pre-assembled and can be set up to be triggered either automatically by a photo cell (which comes with the product) or manually by throwing a switch. The concept is no more complicated than flipping on a light switch. The device is triggered and a red 1.5 volt bulb representing the fusee comes on and begins to flicker realistically just as a real fusee would. The Logic Rail fusee has several nice features such as adjustable flicker rates and burnout times. The burnout time, which can be set at 10 or 20 seconds, is how long it takes the fusee to burn out once the power switch is turned off.

46

In addition to his freight cars, Scott added small magnets to the steps of the locomotives so that the conductor could also be positioned to ride on them.

Scott Thornton

47

Scott added a small steel "foot" to the conductor figure so that the magnet on the car would have something to be attracted to on the plastic figure. He also added a small wire into the back of the figure to act as a handle so that he could easily grab it with a pair of tweezers. *Scott Thornton*

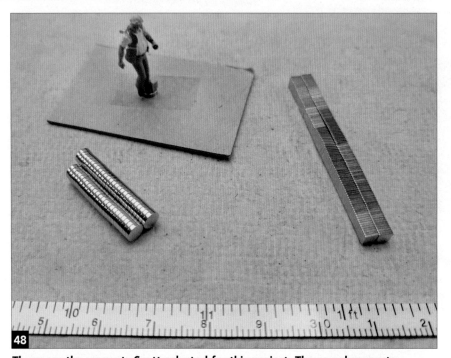

48

These are the magnets Scott selected for this project. The round magnets are for placement along the railroad right-of-way where a conductor could be positioned, and the square neodymium magnets for the cars and locomotives.

Scott Thornton

"I liked this burnout feature so much I began thinking that some sort of delay at the 'lighting' phase would also be a nice way of representing the time it takes for a brakeman to set up and ignite the fusee. I didn't want a situation where a model operator would come upon the crossing, quickly hit a toggle switch, and instantly have the fusees set-up. I wanted to replicate the time it took to set the stage to make the crossing. I considered a few options for modeling the time it would take for the brakeman to set up the fusees. Some of the delay options I considered were adding a countdown delay timer in the circuit, posting written instructions to the crew to wait a specified amount of time, or incorporating some type of removable cover to the toggle switch.

"Ultimately, I settled on a key switch. This is just a basic on/off switch which is flipped by inserting a key and turning it "on." They are relatively inexpensive. I felt this was a good middle ground between the higher cost of timers verses having no manual interaction at all and just using posting crew instructions to 'wait a bit' before flipping the on switch. With the key switch, a crew approaches the crossing, grabs a key mounted on the fascia, inserts it in the switch and turns on the fusee circuit.

"Mounting the board and bulb is a straightforward process. First, a ¹⁄₁₆" inch hole was drilled through my model street at each of the two fusee locations and the 1.2mm fusee bulb inserted in the hole from above, **43**. The 1.2mm bulb fits neatly within the hole and is not particularly noticeable. If you wanted to disguise the bulb when not in use you could position a vehicle or thin manhole cover over it. After I had threaded the bulb through the hole in my street, I inserted it in the connectors on the circuit board as per the Logic Rail instructions.

"Since I didn't have a DC power bus in the vicinity of this particular

49

Scott purchased a pair of tweezers that has a built-in light-emitting diode to assist placing the conductor figure on the cars and locomotives during night operations. *Scott Thornton*

street crossing, I supplied power to the board by tapping my DCC power bus and running wires to the two AC screw terminals on the circuit board. Finally, the key switch was installed in the circuit. Key switches are cylindrical, so I just drilled a hole in my fascia and mounted it in the area of the street crossing, **44**.

"I've been very pleased with the realism of the Logic Rail fusees. My layout isn't particularly large and adding this real world operating procedure adds a few moments to an operating session. At the same time, modeling the fusee set up process doesn't seem too contrived nor does it involve too much head scratching by the switch crew to implement."

Movable conductor figure

Scott Thornton, who models the Milan Branch of the Iowa Interstate Railroad, was looking for a way to incorporate the use a conductor figure into his operations. He wanted an easy way to attach a figure to the sides of a car, **45**, or the steps of a locomotive, **46**. He explored various options and came up with the following solution, the use of

small neodymium magnets and a steel "foot" for the figure.

First, Scott needed to find a good-looking figure set where the models looked like a modern train crew. He found a really nice set of construction workers by Bachmann that fit perfectly. One of the figures looked the most like a modern conductor with a safety vest and holding a radio. Unfortunately, that figure had a dust mask over his face, so he replaced the figures' head with another from the set.

Next, Scott glued a thin, flat piece of steel under the left foot of the conductor. The metal "foot" attached to the conductor has both a front and bottom face, **47**. This way the figure will attach to every car and locomotive with the magnets placed either vertically or horizontally (flat). Scott discovered that using CA for attaching the metal foot to the figure works better than barge cement.

For the locomotives and rolling stock, Scott glued small 3mm neodymium magnets onto each car both on the stirrups or platforms to hold the figure, **48**. Some cars require the magnet be glued to the side of

the car instead of the delicate stirrup step for strength. Scott will paint the magnets to help them blend into the car and disappear. In addition, small round magnets from Super Magnet Man (no. D1021B) will be glued in positions on the layout where the conductor would most likely be on the ground. Scott will then camouflage them with paint and scenery.

Finally, Scott needed a simple way to grab his riding conductor to move him on and off cars and didn't want to use his fingers for fear of damaging delicate details. He found a unique pair of tweezers at Walmart that has a wider spread between the tongs, making for an easier grab, and a built-in LED light, which was perfect because he will be installing blue LEDs for night operations, **49**. Scott glued some soft rubber material on the inside of each tong to protect the conductor figure.

During operations Scott can use the conductor figure to replicate what a prototype conductor would be doing when switching cars. This slows down an ops session and adds a realistic element for the crew to consider.

1

CHAPTER SEVEN

Operating session paperwork

You need to know where the trains are supposed to go, and what to do when they get there

A two person crew, Cody Akers, left, as conductor, and Ralph Schiring as the engineer, operate the local on Joe Atkinson's Iowa Interstate Railroad, Subdivision 4, West End. The conductor refers to the switch list and coordinates the switching movements with the engineer. This allows the engineer to concentrate on operating the locomotive realistically using the ProtoThrottle. *Joe Atkinson*

Once you get your layout built, it is time to begin holding operating sessions. They can range from being very informal, such as switching a few cars by yourself, to having several friends come over for a multi-hour ops session, **1**. As soon as you invite the first guest operator over, you'll need some kind of paperwork to indicate the work to be done during the ops session.

2

Delaware-Lackawanna train dispatcher Dave Crosby keys up the mike to issue a verbal authority to a train crew. *Samantha Kuczynski*

3

Tony Koester's Allegheny Midland was radio-dispatched using this Union Switch & Signal CTC machine, built from SP parts by Rod Loder, by hanging markers on the levers to show train-authority limits. It was never hard-wired. *Tony Koester*

Types of paperwork

Prototype railroads rely on paperwork and computer systems to keep the trains moving and operating safely. Without it, the railroad grinds to a halt. While railroads have numerous types of forms and paperwork we'll focus on the ones that move trains from one location to another and switch individual cars in this chapter.

For our purposes, we'll divide the paperwork into two categories, those that give trains permission to operate, and those that indicate the destination of cars. For any train or on-track-equipment (OTE) to occupy a main line where other trains or OTE operates, the crew is required to receive authority from a control station or dispatcher, **2**. This authority can be issued as a clearance card, track warrant, block sheet, or one of the other forms prototype railroads use or have used to grant authority to crews. In addition, another type of control known as Centralized Traffic Control (CTC) can be used in which train movements are authorized by signals that permit movement, **3**. Each type of authority has numerous rules and requirements that cover its use. Tony Koester's *Realistic Model Railroad Operation, Second Edition* by Kalmbach Publishing, and *A Compendium of Model Railroad Operations—From Design to Implementation* by the Operations Special Interest Group (OpSIG) are excellent resources to get more information on these different types of operational authority systems.

In this chapter we'll discuss the most common types of paperwork used on model railroads and how it can be applied to a small switching layout. The paperwork can be as simple or complex as you want—it all depends on your layout and how many trains you plan to run at a time.

Operational rules handout

One of the first documents you should develop is an operational rules handout for your layout. This handout should list all the rules that apply to your model railroad and indicate how you want your railroad operated.

The handout should also include any special instructions that pertain to operating your layout. It is important to remember that first-time visitors to your layout may not be familiar with your operating system, car switching paperwork, and the rules that you have established. The operational rules handout should outline those items in a brief format and help new visitors successfully operate your model railroad.

First-time guests to my layout receive a copy of a GNRR Operating Rules handout. These rules describe the railroad operating procedures and help guide them as to how to prototypically operate my model railroad.

The document was developed and based on one that replicates the prototype Georgia Northeastern Railroad Timetable for all employees. The timetable describes special situations and updates to the standard GNRR Operating Rules book. The timetable document was modified and combined with the GNRR Operating Rules book into an Operating Rules handout that covers the most important prototype rules and procedures for my layout, **4**.

The goal of the Operating Rules document is not to provide so many rules and procedures that it becomes a deterrent to an enjoyable operations session, but that it gives operators a structure in which to experience a prototype-based operating session. The document helps guests better understand the prototype procedures and feel comfortable operating on my layout. The most important rules are for guests to relax, have fun, and enjoy operating on the layout.

Movement authority

All trains need authority to occupy a main line. The type of system used to determine that authority is dependent on the era modeled and the type of authority system chosen by the layout owner. The most common types of authority systems are Centralized Traffic Control (CTC), Automatic Block Signals (ABS), Track Warrant Control (TWC), Direct Traffic Control (DTC), Verbal Block System (VBS), and Timetable and Train Orders (TTTO).

In a CTC system, a clearance card or train clearance is issued establishing the train's identity or symbol. Once in

Georgia Northeastern Railroad

Operating Rules

Effective June 8, 2013

CTC territory, crews follow signals that display aspects that direct movement. Signals and switches are controlled from a remote location by a dispatcher who controls all train movement and determines priorities for each train. All trains are of equal status and operate based on signal indications that permit movement, **5**.

Rules and signal indications in CTC territory are extensive and those model railroaders who operate under this type of control system must have a thorough understanding of the signals and the actions that need to be taken to comply with the signals. This type of system is best suited to larger layouts that have a significant distance between towns or stations.

Automatic Block Signals

In most cases, an Automatic Block Signal (ABS) system is not an authority system, but an automatic signal control system that indicates the condition of the track ahead. The system conveys this information about the condition of the track within the block with automatic line side signals displayed to the train crews. Trains operating in an ABS system still need the permission of a control station or dispatcher to authorize their movement. This permission can be given as a track warrant or a track authority form. A timetable schedule or train order can also authorize movement. A Clearance Form A essentially authorizes movement through ABS territory for a scheduled train as long as the block is clear, as does a Form A with a train order.

For an ABS system to operate, the railroad divides the rail line into sections or "blocks" indicated by signals at the beginning of each block. Crews must be familiar with the locations of the signals that control each block.

The ABS system detects track occupancy through the use of an electric circuit. If the block is occupied, it activates the appropriate trackside signal, and those in advance of the block, indicating a stop or a restriction. The system can also detect breaks in the rails or improperly lined switches to prevent accidents.

This system permits trains to follow each other in the same direction and maintain safe spacing between them, **6**.

The Georgia Northeastern Railroad (GNRR) is a prototype short line that operates between Marietta, GA and Copperhill, TN. This model railroad replicates portions of the line from Elizabeth Yard in Marietta, GA to the branch line from Tate, GA to Marble Hill. The primary goal of the operating session is to have fun and enjoy your time operating on my GNRR layout.

I. METHOD OF OPERATION

1. **Movement Authority**-All trains must contact the control station before occupying any non-controlled tracks and trains will be governed by verbal instructions of the control station. Such system will constitute a Verbal Block System (VBS). An Absolute Block may be occupied by only one train at a time which allows movement in any direction. Crews will sign out for a block prior to departing and sign in the block when completed.

2. **VBS Block Limits**-
   Marietta Block from Elizabeth Yard to Highway 53.
   Tate Block from Highway 53 to Long Swamp Creek bridge.
   Marble Hill Block from derail on Marble Hill lead to end of the line track bumper in Marble Hill.

II. SPEEDS

1. Maximum Authorized Speed is 10 MPH.
2. Maximum speed for coupling is 3 MPH

III. TRAIN CREW INSTRUCTIONS

1. The Conductor shall refer to the Switch List to determine which cars need to be pulled or spotted.
2. The Conductor shall coordinate all movements and direct the Engineer in pulling and spotting cars.

Page 2

---

3. The Conductor shall provide verbal instructions to the Engineer indicating the distance in car lengths and/or feet to stopping or coupling.
4. The Conductor shall provide point protection for all shove moves and verify switches are properly lined.
5. The Conductor shall request "Red Zone" prior to placing themselves in a fouling position on or between equipment.

IV. INSTRUCTIONS RELATING TO OPERATING RULES

1. **Hazardous Materials Placement**- Placarded loaded hazardous materials cars must be separated by at least one car from the locomotive. See Switch List for cars indicated "HZ".
2. **Grade Crossings**- Grade crossings may not be blocked for more than 10 fast clock minutes. No cars shall be left less than 50' away from any grade crossing.
3. **Switches**- The normal position for switches is for straight away movement and shall be lined in that position when not in use.
4. **Derails**- The normal position of derails is in the derailing position and shall be returned to normal when not in use.
5. **Clearance Point Indicators**- A yellow painted tie indicates the clearance point for equipment on all sidings.
6. **Blue Flags**- Blue signals displayed signify that workmen are on, under, or between rolling stock. When displayed the equipment must not be coupled to and must be removed only by the same craft or group that displayed them.
7. **Headlights**- The headlight must be displayed "bright" on the leading end of every train. *Function F0 controls the headlight.*
8. **Bell**- The engine bell must be rung when an engine is about to move, except after momentary stops in continuous switching movements. It must be rung while approaching and passing through grade crossings. *Function F1 controls the bell.*

Page 3

---

9. **Horn Signals**- The horn shall be sounded approaching all grade crossings. The sounding of the horn with two long, one short, and one long blast shall be sounded before entering the crossing with the last long blast prolonged until the locomotive occupies the crossing. *Function F2 controls the horn.*
10. **Whistle Post Signs**- A whistle post sign indicated with a "W" are located approximately three cars lengths away from all grade crossings.
11. **Ditch Lights**- Ditch lights shall be illuminated on the locomotive when traveling on the main line and through all grade crossings. *Function F6 controls the ditch lights.*
12. **End of Train (EOT) Protection**- A flag or EOT device shall be attached to the last car in the train to provide end of train protection.
13. **Facility fence gates**- Gates are normally in the closed position. The crew shall open the gate prior to entering the siding for that facility. Control panels for the gate are located on the fascia and indicate the proper direction to turn the handle to open. Stop when the gate reaches the full open or closed position. Crews shall close the gate once switching is completed and the siding switch is returned to normal.
14. **Overhead rolling doors**- Two industries are equipped with operating overhead rolling doors. Crews shall open the door by turning the operating knob disguised as a roof top ventilator counterclockwise to open the door. Stop once the door is fully opened.
15. **Shove moves at enclosed facilities**- When shoving into all buildings, movement must be stopped before entering and the crew must ascertain that all equipment is clear before spotting/pulling cars.

Page 4

4

This GNRR Operating Rules handout is distributed to all new operators on Tom's layout. The document highlights the rules and procedures he encourages operators to follow during an ops session.

The CTC signals in Coosa Pines, Ala., on the CSX Lineville Subdivision line from Birmingham, Ala., to Manchester, Ga., are controlled by a dispatcher working in Jacksonville, Fla.

The Rock Island crew has stopped for a red ABS signal on Mike Armstrong's layout. Working signals add a prototypical control element to an ops session as crews must observe and obey the signals during their runs. *Mike Armstrong*

Model railroaders can incorporate this type of signaling system on their model railroad. A model railroad must be divided into blocks for an ABS system to work properly. Track occupancy detection circuits can sense the presence of train in a specified block.

Some detection circuits require a resistor be soldered on the wheel sets of cars so the system can sense cars occupying a block in addition to the locomotives.

Crews must have an understanding of the proper actions to take based on signal indication, and that they still need authority from a control station, dispatcher, or timetable for their movement. For more about signal systems, see *Model Railroader's Guide to Signals & Interlockings* by Dave Abeles from Kalmbach Books.

Track Warrant Control

Track warrants are a method of providing authority for trains to operate by providing instructions specifying movements on a pre-printed form, **7**. A dispatcher will issue a track warrant to a crew via radio or phone. The crew will copy the information provided by the dispatcher onto a track warrant form and will read it back to verify understanding. Once the dispatcher confirms the track warrant is correct, he or she will issue an OK time and the dispatcher's name.

Track warrants differ slightly from direct traffic control as they will indicate specific reference points and not necessary blocks. A track warrant can specify movement between any points specifically identified on the track warrant. In addition, they can relay other special instructions to the train crews.

Track warrants will generally follow a standard form specified by the General Code of Operating Rules. A track warrant will normally be issued for movement in one direction, but they can allow movement in any direction if the Work Between box is checked, **8**. In this situation, only one train can be authorized to occupy that specific section of the railroad at a time, although certain circumstances are allowed by the rule book to permit two or more trains within the same limits.

As trains progress along their route, they advise the dispatcher they have cleared the specified locations and then additional track warrants can be issued.

This type of authority system works well for unsignaled (dark) territory on our model railroads. Depending on the amount of traffic, a full-time dispatcher position may be needed to control the movements of all trains. The person in this role must have a good understanding of the rules and regulations regarding issuing track warrants. The drawback to this type of system is the short distances on

Track Warrant

NO. _____		, 19 ___
To: _____	At: _____	

1.	☐	Track Warrant NO. _____ Is Void.
2.	☐	Proceed From _____ To _____ On _____ Track.
3.	☐	Proceed From _____ To _____ On _____ Track.
4.	☐	Work Between _____ And _____ On _____ Track.
5.	☐	Not In Effect Until _____
6.	☐	This Authority Expires At _____
7.	☐	Not in Effect Until After Arrival Of _____ At _____
8.	☐	Hold Main Track At Last Named Point.
9.	☐	Do Not Foul Limits Ahead Of _____
10.	☐	Clear Main Track At Last Named Point.
11.	☐	Between _____ And _____ Make All Movements At Restricted Speed. Limits Occupied By Train.
12.	☐	Between _____ And _____ Make All Movements At Restricted Speed. Limits Occupied By Men Or Equipment.
13.	☐	Do Not Exceed _____ MPH Between _____ And _____
14.	☐	Do Not Exceed _____ MPH Between _____ And _____
15.	☐	Flag Protection Not Required Against Following Trains On The Same Track.
16.	☐	Track Bulletins In Effect ____, ____, ____,
17.	☐	Other Specific Instructions: _____

OK _____	Dispatcher _____
Relayed To _____	Copied By _____
Limits Reported Clear At _____	By _____

7

A track warrant form is used by railroads to control the movement of trains. A dispatcher will issue a track warrant and the crew will copy the information on the form, checking the appropriate boxes and filling in the information on the form. The crew will read back the track warrant to the dispatcher to verify understanding before the dispatcher issues an OK time and his or her name.

our model railroads can lead to an overwhelming workload as a dispatcher issues track warrants for each train crew.

Direct Traffic Control

As railroads migrated away from timetable and train orders to other

8

Checking the WORK BETWEEN box on the track warrant form allows the local crew to make the necessary moves in any direction to switch the cars. Once it has completed its work, the crew will contact the dispatcher to notify him or her that the crew has cleared the specified points. *James McNab*

9

A sign trackside indicates the beginning of a block on the Georgia Northeastern Railroad. A dispatcher will authorize all movements within the specified block.

GNRR Georgia Northeastern Railroad

BLOCK SHEET FOR TRAIN, OTE OR EMPLOYEE IN CHARGE

DATE: 9-6-13   TIMETABLE IN EFFECT / 8   BULLETIN IN EFFECT / 4

Train, OTE or Employee in Charge	Block or Blocks Received	Type of Block Direction	Time Received	Dispatcher Initials	Block or Blocks Cleared	Time Cleared	Dispatcher Initials
E. Dalrymple	BR	A	1020 T	JS			
	MC	A	1020	JS			

NOTE: When receiving blocks by a transfer, put an (*) where dispatcher's initials go and note the transfer on the bottom of the page.

TRANSFER SHEET

Train, OTE or Employee in Charge	Block or Blocks Transferred	Type of Block	According to Rule	Transfer To	Transfer Time	Transfer Date
					T	
					T	

NOTES

Received Transfer from Central Station 11 Cars 2 loco on main

10

A block sheet is used to record the issuing of a block(s) to a train crew, on track equipment (OTE), or employee in charge. The employee will record the block(s) issued (a two letter abbreviation of the block name), type of block direction, time received, and the dispatcher's initials. Here the dispatcher has issued two "A" (Absolute) blocks, BR and MC, to engineer E. Dalrymple at 10:20 a.m.

authority systems, the concept of Direct Traffic Control (DTC) was developed. The DTC system utilizes the concept of blocks to control movements. A block is a designated section of track identified by signs at the beginning of each block, **9**. Similar to a TWC system, a control station or dispatcher authorizes train movements by issuing specified instructions. The difference is that under DTC the block limits are specified in the timetable and authority can only be issued for the designated blocks, while TWC can authorize movements between any specified points on the railroad. In DTC only one train may be authorized to occupy a block at a time.

Verbal Block System

A Verbal Block System (VBS) is used by the Georgia Northeastern Railroad to control the movement of trains and on-track equipment (OTE). Verbal Block System rules do not apply within yard limits. This authority system is version of DTC.

A control station will grant one of the following types of blocks for trains in a VBS:

Absolute Block: A block that may

be occupied by only one train or OTE at a time.

Occupied Block: A block clear of opposing trains or OTE, but not necessarily clear of preceding or standing trains or OTE.

An Absolute Block authority will be granted for movements in both directions, while an Occupied Block authority will be granted for movements in one direction, which must be specified. Trains or OTE must not enter a block until the engineer or employee in charge has received authority to do so from the control station, **10**.

This type of authority system works well for unsignaled model railroads and those with limited operations. Crew members are authorized to operate within a specified block(s) by a control station or dispatcher and sign-in on a block sheet with the time and date. Once their work is complete, they notify the control station or dispatcher that they have cleared the block and it can be signed out and released. As on the prototype, a train crew must not report "Clear" until all the switches and/or derails have been locked and lined back to the normal position.

Timetable and Train Orders

One of the oldest forms of authority, dating to the mid-1800s, is timetable and train orders (TTTO). In this authority system, a timetable is published with all the regularly scheduled trains listed, **11**. A dispatcher issues a clearance card, **12**, that authorizes movement for a train based on the timetable. In addition, train orders can be issued that modify or amend the timetable, **13**.

Extra trains, those not listed in the timetable, can be authorized to operate and must coordinate their movements with the scheduled trains. Superiority of trains is determined by right, class, or direction. The superior direction east/west or north/south is determined by each railroad and is found in the railroad's special instructions.

Operating on a model railroad that utilizes TTTO operation places a lot of responsibility on the crews to determine their movements. Crews

The Tri-State Model Railroads club (TSMRI.org) uses timetable and train orders (TTTO) for operating sessions on the L&N "Old Line" layout. Crews must be familiar with the TTTO rules and understand how to read a timetable when operating the layout.

A Santa Fe Clearance Card Form 902 is issued to train crews on Jared Harper's layout. The clearance card, when completed, gives the crew authorization to operate on the Alma Branch line.

must be familiar with all the rules that pertain to operating and have a knowledge of the time limits and distances between the stations. The OpSIG book *19 East, Copy Three* covers in great detail the rules and procedures that apply to TTTO operations.

Other types of authority

One of the simplest forms of authority can be found if there is no main line designated. Some industrial areas and locations specified as auxiliary tracks or tracks other than the main track operate under restricted speed requirements, **14**. Restricted speed limits may vary by railroad, but typically the maximum speed limit is no more than 20 mph. Crews are required to be able to stop short of a train or engine, improperly lined switch, derail, or any other obstruction. In many locations this may severely limit a trains' speed,

Form 19	Form 19

L&N   **TSMRI**

Train Order No _____   Date:_____
- -
To C & E

_____ at _____
_____ at _____
_____ at _____
_____ at _____
- -
Instructions:

_____

Repeated and complete time _____ M _____ Opr.

13   Form 19 Rev 02

14

This Train Order Sheet (Form 19) from the Tri-State Model Railroad club is used by the dispatcher to issue train orders to the crews operating on the layout. Any employee or train that is affected by the train order must receive a copy. Each train order must be given in the same words to all employees or trains addressed.

The joint CSX and Norfolk Southern operation at the Coosa Pines Industrial Park was designated as auxiliary tracks, and locomotives operated under restricted speed requirements, not exceeding 10 mph. Train movements were governed by auxiliary track rules, and did not require a movement authority. *Tom Holley*

as in some yards and industrial plants visibility is limited.

Within yard limits with a main line, crews can operate under restricted speed requirements and may occupy the main without authorization, while still observing the restricted speed, except for clearing the main line for scheduled first class trains in the TTTO era, **15**. If the yard has no main line designated, then all trains operate under restricted speed requirements, usually not exceeding 10 mph.

For small switching layouts, designating an area as falling under one of the above categories allows crews to move without a formal authorization. While they still must follow the rules regarding moving under restricted sped, crews do not have to receive a track warrant or other form of approval to operate.

Job aids
One type of paperwork that is helpful to new operators on your layout is a

job aid form. While this form may not have a prototypical counterpart, it is very useful for operators to understand the work required for each job on your model railroad.

A job aid should be included with the paperwork given to a crew when it receives its train authorization and car switching information. The form indicates the steps needed to complete the yard switch job, local, through freight, or passenger train.

It is easy for layout owners to know what each job is and how it is to be done, but many times they overlook that kind of information for new operators and they need to explain that to guests in a simplified format. Having a job aid reduces confusion and questions to the layout owner on how a job should be performed.

On my CSX Hawksridge Division layout, I developed a job aid form for each job assignment on the railroad. The form was printed on a half sheet of 8½" x 11" paper with the switch list on the other half, **16**. The crew could simply follow the instructions on the job aid and successfully complete the work even if it was their first time visiting the layout.

Car movement paperwork
Now that we have discussed the types of authority to operate the trains we'll discuss the second part of the operating session paperwork, the car destination section, **17**. There are several different systems model railroaders use to assign destinations for their cars. The most common systems are car cards/waybills (CC/WB) and switch lists. Each system has its own advantages and disadvantages, and can be a topic of great debate among modelers as to which system is best. In this chapter we'll highlight each method, and discuss a few variations of each system.

Car cards
One of the most popular car movement systems is the Micro-Mark Car Routing System. Doug Smith introduced modelers to two-cycle waybills that slipped into pockets on cards in the 1960s. Old Line Graphics, and later Micro-Mark, then produced smaller (2" x 4") four-cycle versions of the car card/waybill system. Micro-Mark offers a Starter Pack (no. 82916) that contains everything you need to get started, **18**. Additional components

15 The designated main line through Elizabeth Yard on the L&N "Old Line" is easy to identify with the light gray ballast as compared to the black cinder ballast in the yard. Within yard limits, crews may occupy the main without authorization, except for clearing the main for scheduled first class trains in the TTTO era.

and forms are available separately for purchase if needed.

To use the Micro-Mark system you begin by filling out a car card for every car in your fleet. The car card contains the KIND, AAR code, RAILROAD or CAR OWNER and NUMBER, and a brief DESCRIPTION (usually the color) of the car. Locomotives cards are also filled out in the same manner. The EMPTY CAR RETURN TO section on the car card is also completed, indicating a location that the car should be routed to when empty. After filling out the car information, the flap is folded up and taped to the card creating a pocket for the waybill.

Once the car cards are filled out it is time to complete the waybills. The Micro-Mark system uses a four-cycle waybill with two destinations on each side of the waybill. The waybill has blank lines for the CONSIGNEE, ADDRESS, ROUTING, VIA, SHIPPER, and LADING. The layout owner then fills out the information for each waybill for destinations on his or her layout and off-site destinations (staging). The information needed for each waybill can be extensive, based on how prototypical you want to be. Many

modelers use prototype information gained from numerous sources to fill out the waybills, **19**.

To hold the car cards and waybills, bill boxes are placed on the fascia near yards, stations, and switching areas. Each slot in the bill box has an industry or track name for the car cards that correspond to the cars on that track. Some owners will provide a separate bill box slot for inbound, outbound, and

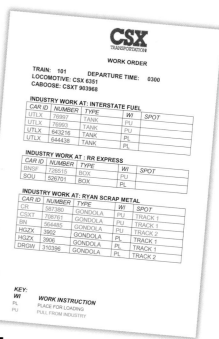

16 A job aid is provided with the switch list (work order) for each job on Tom's previous CSX Hawksridge Subdivision layout. The job aid provided information and instructions to the switch crews on where to pick up their locomotives, train cars, and the work to be performed along the route.

A local train approaches the yard to set out its cars. Some type of car destination routing system is needed to specify where the cars go and which cars need to be picked up if we are going to have operating sessions on our layouts.

holds for each industry, **20**.

Before an ops session, the layout owner checks all the car cards and waybill destinations for each car, turning any waybills to change their destination if necessary. If a car is empty, the waybill can be changed indicating a location that the empty car should be returned to.

As crews pick up their trains, they also pick up the car cards for each car in their trains. The crew will note the destination for each car and arrange the cars in the consist (unless the yard crew has already blocked the cars) to place blocks of cars for the same destination together.

Once the local crew departs the yard, it sets out cars at the designated locations indicated on the waybills, and also checks the bill boxes for outbound cars that need to be picked up. The crew will also place the inbound car card with its waybill in the correct box at the industry.

After the crew arrives at its final destination, it places the car cards in the appropriate bill box for the yard or staging track. Yard crews classify

the cars, making up outbound and local trains based on the waybills. Overlays slipped in front of the waybill can reroute cars to icing platforms, livestock watering facilities, and other destinations.

The benefit of the car card/waybill system is that it is endless once you have the car cards and waybills completed. The layout owner only has to turn the waybills to begin the next session. Many modelers are familiar with the system so training guests how to use it are limited to first-time or inexperienced operators.

The disadvantages are if a car card is lost or misplaced, it causes problems until it can be located. The car card and waybill system was adapted to fit the needs of model railroaders and does not replicate the forms used by prototype crews. Even with these disadvantages, it remains a very popular way to manage car movements.

Realistic-format waybills

Recently, Tony Thompson, Tony Koester, Ted Pamperin, John King, and perhaps others have developed same-

size waybills that fit into the old bill boxes, but are much more realistic in appearance, **21**. They are completely interchangeable with the four-cycle waybills and therefore can replace them incrementally. Instead of car cards, the bills are slipped into clear plastic sleeves and stacked one atop another like playing cards inside the sleeves.

The bills can be printed on standard copy paper, and therefore as few as one to as many as eight waybills can be stacked in a plastic sleeve. The bills are cycled by moving the bill on the bottom of the "deck" to the top.

Overlays such as Empty Car Orders can route empty cars ("MTYs") to industries for loading or refrigerator cars to icing platforms for icing. Cars are "loaded" at industries by adding waybills stored in each industry's bill box. Tony Koester covers in greater detail the realistic-format waybills in the second edition of his Kalmbach book, *Realistic Model Railroad Operation*.

Switch lists

The second way to indicate car destinations is by using switch lists.

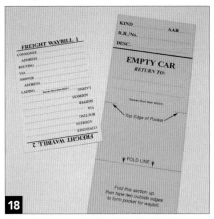

18 The Micro-Mark Car Routing System has car cards that you fill out for each car in your roster. The four cycle waybills are completed to route the cars to different locations, staging, or industries on the layout.

19 A completed waybill is inserted into the car card sleeve. The freight waybill shows this Santa Fe automobile boxcar is on its way west to Los Angeles with a load of Buicks. When the waybill is turned to Step 4, it will send the now empty car back east for another load. *Andy Sperandeo*

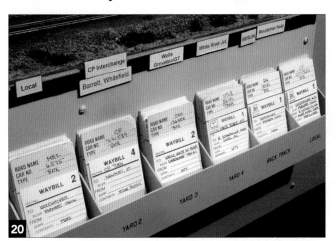

20 This yard file box has a card pocket for each track, with each track labeled on the front of the pocket. Tags on the magnetic strip above the cards show the destination blocks assembled on each track. As seen in the case of Yard 2, more than one block can occupy the same track. *Paul Dolkos*

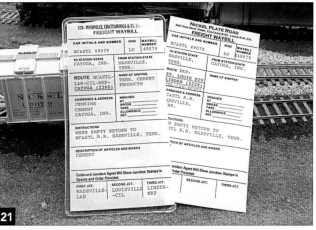

21 This Nashville, Chattanooga & St. Louis covered hopper (AAR car type LO) was routed via the Louisville & Nashville, Monon (CI&L), and the Nickel Plate Road to Jenkins Cement at Cayuga, Ind., on an NC&StL waybill. It will return to home rails via the reverse route on a NKP waybill. Tony Koester made the waybill as a Word document. The blue typeface represents a typewriter ribbon. Note the typing is in all caps. *Tony Koester*

These lists can be filled out by hand using a blank form, typed up on a computer, or auto-generated based on parameters in a car movement computer program.

When talking to prototype crew members about switching, they all indicate they need to know three things when it comes to car movement: the cars' reporting marks and number, where is it going, and if it a hazardous materials car that needs special handling or placement in their train, **22**. Switch lists vary slightly from one

railroad to another, but they all contain this information.

A simplified switch list can be made for your layout that has the above information. The list should include all the industries the crew will encounter on its local job and the cars in its train, **23**. Cars listed under each industry as "place" are the cars that are in the train consist when the crew initially departs the yard.

On Jared Harper's Santa Fe Alma Branch, he fills out a switch list by hand on a prototypical Santa Fe

Switch List form. Crews then use the list to determine the outbound cars to be picked up and the destinations of inbound cars, **24**.

When developing a switch list for my GNRR layout, I looked to the prototype to see what form was used and determine if it would work for my layout. I was able to obtain copies of the GNRR prototype forms it used and developed a similar switch list form on an Excel spreadsheet, **25**.

The switch list indicates all the cars in the train, which is in staging, in the

WORK ORDER

TRAIN: DEPARTURE TIME:
LOCOMOTIVE:
CABOOSE:

INDUSTRY WORK AT:

CAR ID	NUMBER	TYPE	WI	SPOT

INDUSTRY WORK AT :

CAR ID	NUMBER	TYPE	WI	SPOT

INDUSTRY WORK AT:

CAR ID	NUMBER	TYPE	WI	SPOT

KEY:
WI   WORK INSTRUCTION
PL   PLACE FOR LOADING
PU   PULL FROM INDUSTRY

23 A simplified switch list can be made on a computer and filled out by hand. The list should include all the industries served on the specific switch job. Cars listed as Places (set outs) at each industry are the cars in the train consist when the crew initially departs the yard or staging.

22 A railroad conductor needs to know a car's reporting marks and number, where is it going, and if it is a hazardous materials car that requires special handling. All of that information can be found on the switch list. Note the folded switch list in the conductor's back pocket along with his switch lock key hanging from his belt. Those are the two most important items he needs to do his work.

order from the locomotive to the end of the train.

This part of the form is essentially a "Wheel Report," which indicates all the cars in the train. The cars are blocked by industry, but not necessarily in the correct order for spotting. The industry that each car is routed to is listed on the line with the car information under the "Block To" column.

The next section of the switch list indicates all the industries and sidings as you proceed from South to North. The cars that need to be picked up will indicate CSX Elizabeth Yard (CSXT ELI), under the Block To column, which is staging. Cars staying (holds), will have the industry listed under the Block To column. Some cars will need to be moved and re-spotted to pull cars that need to be picked up.

The other information on the switch list indicates the type of car, commodity or empty, and the weight. The weight is not critical for the operating session, but just makes the list look more prototypical.

Several different operating sessions are pre-formatted and new ones can easily be made by changing the car numbers and locations to make a different session. The combinations are endless so each session can be different. The switch list is not auto-generated, so I can control the number of cars going to each industry and to be picked up for each ops session. The car frequency for each industry is based on information gathered from the prototype crews.

On one industry on my GNRR layout, Dow Chemical, the switching instructions indicate a specific spot for the inbound car, **26**. Each tank car must go to a specific spot for unloading, and that can mean a lot more work for the crew.

On the prototype, the crew may have to move partially unloaded cars at Dow, spot them on a siding outside of the facility, and then re-spot the car at the facility on another day when they need the chemical again. This same procedure can be replicated on my layout every few ops sessions, as it adds additional steps for the crews.

Tim Garland, a Norfolk Southern engineer, uses switch lists for his Seaboard Central layout based on the forms he uses every day on the job. The forms have an alphanumeric code assigned for each industry. The switch list has each of the industries listed for the switch job and the instruction column indicates if a car is pulled or placed. In addition, cars that are being picked up list a destination code for a specified yard, such as Birmingham (BHAM), so that the cars can be placed in the proper yard track, **27**.

A separate form, a track inventory sheet, indicates all the cars in the yard in order on each yard track, **28**. Crews use this form to locate the cars needed for their trains. Tim inputs the information into a spreadsheet program and prints out new forms before each ops session. The form is not auto-generated, so he can specify what cars he wants to switch each ops session.

JMRI switch list program

Many model railroaders are familiar with the Java Model Railroad Interface (JMRI) program which offers a suite of programs including DecoderPro, PanelPro, DispatcherPro, OperationsPro, and SoundPro. Java Model Railroad Interface is available as a free download at jmri.org and can be run on computers that have the Java program installed. The two most popular programs are DecoderPro, for programming DCC decoders, and PanelPro, which provides computer control for layouts. As an open-source project, the program is constantly being updated and revised by dedicated model railroaders who contribute to the JMRI program.

Within the PanelPro portion of the JMRI program is the OperationsPro program, which allows model railroaders to develop computer-generated switch lists. This feature provides a different approach to running a model railroad than using

24 Jared Harper uses a prototypical Santa Fe switch list for car movement operations on his layout. The list is filled out by Jared prior to the ops session. Towns are identified on the left hand margin, with the cars to be switched on the lines to the right. The terms "take" and "leave" in the Remarks column, as opposed to pull and spot, are based on information obtained by interviewing the prototype crew that worked the line.

car cards and waybills. Like the prototype, OperationsPro allows the use of the computer to decide how freight cars are moved around the layout. To use this program, a number of layout attributes, such as towns, industries, yards, rolling stock, train routes and trains need to be defined. Extensive instructions on using and setting up OperationsPro can be found on the JMRI website under the OperationsPro tab.

25 The switch lists for Tom's layout are based on the prototype forms used by the Georgia Northeastern Railroad (GNRR). The cars for the North Local No. 101 to be set out at the industries are listed at the top of the form under the Elizabeth Yard section. Industries are listed in station order from south to north, and cars at each industry requiring pick up are listed in the "Block To" column as CSXT ELI, indicating for them to be taken by the local to the GNRR interchange with CSX in Elizabeth Yard.

26

27

Tim Garland uses a switch list that he made on an Excel spread sheet that closely resembles the prototype switch list used by Norfolk Southern. The list has each industry listed and indicates each car that is to be pulled or placed under the "INST" column for that industry.

28

The Track Inventory Switch list indicates all the cars in the yard on each track and their destination. Cars listed on SY02 for Griffin are to be switched to the local industries. Each industry has an alphanumeric identification number listed under the "CLASSCD" column, which helps crews identify its location.

Dow chemical is a spot-specific industry. The specific unloading spot is listed in the "Switch Inst." column on the switch list. This adds extra work for the local crew as some cars may need to be pulled and re-spotted to access one requiring pickup.

Here we'll outline the basic steps that need to be taken to set up the operations switch list—or manifest as JMRI calls them—generating program. As with most computer programs, there is a learning curve, but help is available through an online group, JMRI Users Group at Groups. io. The best way to learn is to begin experimenting with the program with a simple setup and see what it will do, and if you run into problems, ask for help on the online forum group.

The first step is to download the current Production Release of the JMRI program appropriate for your computer system from the website, jmri.org. Once the program has been downloaded and installed, select the PanelPro program to begin setting up the attributes for OperationsPro. In the PanelPro tool bar select the

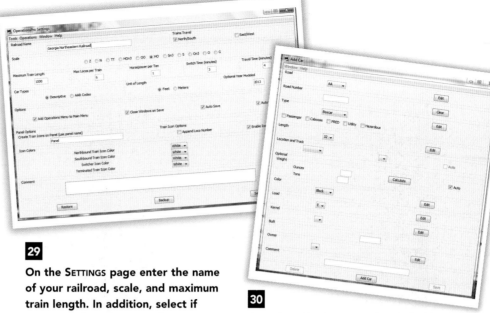

29

On the SETTINGS page enter the name of your railroad, scale, and maximum train length. In addition, select if you want the ARR car codes or a description for your cars. Once you have all the fields completed, click the SAVE button.

30

Complete the CAR page for each car in your fleet. The car type can be edited and different car descriptions added if needed.

TOOLS> OPERATIONS> SETTINGS. On the SETTINGS page you will want to name your railroad, set the scale, and maximum train length. Also decide what directions you need your traffic to flow. Most layouts will have just two directions, east/west or north/south, but if you have a complex layout you may need both. Also decide whether you want to use a description (e.g. Boxcar) or AAR Codes (e.g. XM) for your rolling stock. In the OPTIONS section be sure to select the ADD OPERATIONS MENU TO MAIN MENU option if you will be using OperationsPro frequently. Once you have completed this page, click the save button, **29**.

It is recommended you complete the remaining dropdown categories under the OPERATIONS tab in the order they appear. The next category is LOCATIONS. This is cities, towns, or yard areas on your layout where trains originate or do work. Enter the name of the town or yard and click on the ADD LOCATION button at the bottom of the screen.

Once you have the name entered, it

will take you back to the same screen and you can now select the rolling stock served by the location. Whatever you select here will be available for further filtering at the industry spurs or yards in this location.

You must then define the tracks at this location. Here you can select if the track is a SPUR, YARD, CLASSIFICATION/INTERCHANGE, or STAGING track. For JMRI purposes, spurs are where freight cars are worked, so a loaded car changes to empty, or an empty one is loaded. The program does this automatically after a dwell time.

YARDS and CLASSIFICATION/ INTERCHANGE YARDS are where trains are broken down, or assembled without their load status changing.

STAGING is used to hold complete trains, no changing of loads takes place, and no breakdown of trains occurs there.

The most important part of the TRACK settings is the length. This represents the track available for placing freight cars at the industry or spur, not the actual track length. In fact a siding can be defined as multiple SPUR TRACKS, if there is more than one industry or spot for cars.

In the CARS section you will build a roster of all your rolling stock, **30**.

Click on the ADD button and complete all the fields on the screen. Once you have all the fields completed, click on the ADD CAR button at the bottom of the screen.

An optional section is for LOCOMOTIVES. This is used if you want the JMRI program to assign locomotives to your trains. If you want to determine the locomotives independently of the program you can leave this section blank. If you use the DecoderPro part of JMRI for programming your DCC decoders, then you can import your locomotive roster from that part of JMRI.

Before defining TRAINS, you need to specify the routes the trains will use on the ROUTES tab. Click on the ADD ROUTE button and then select the starting location of the train.

Complete the remaining information on the location line indicating direction, pickups, setouts, etc. Add other locations as required and complete the required fields. Note that for a route that is used for a "turn train," i.e. a train that goes from A to B and then back to A, the route is defined as A-B-B-A, as the first B represents the end of the outgoing leg and the second B is for the start of the return leg. OperationsPro recognizes this structure and does

SWITCHLIST FOR YARD CREW		PAGE - 1 -		2/2/2020 9:58

YARD CREW ONLY   L&N TSMRI

TSMRI-L&N OLD LINE

YARD WORK FOR ELIZABETH

TRAIN #44
TRAIN ORIGINATES HERE, DEPARTURE: 13:01

[X]	Action	Road	Number	Type	Color	Track	Dest./(Load)	Final Dest
( )	PULL	CG	6001	BOXCAR	RED	LIZ TRK 2	TATE	LOWER MTN COAL&SUPPLY
( )	PULL	PRR	85328	BOXCAR	RED	LIZ YARD TRKS	ELLIJAY	
( )	PULL	SHPX	10169	TANK OIL	BLACK	LIZ YARD TRKS	ELLIJAY	
( )	PULL	CB&Q	188734	GONDOLA	RED	LIZ TRK 2	BLUE RIDGE	
( )	PULL	LN	49409	GONDOLA	BROWN	LIZ TRK 2	BLUE RIDGE	
( )	PULL	CB&Q	188080	GONDOLA	BROWN	LIZ TRK 2	BLUE RIDGE	
( )	PULL	SAL	22209	BOXCAR	BROWN	LIZ TRK 2	MURPHY JUNCTION	
( )	PULL	NW	49300	BOXCAR	BROWN	LIZ TRK 2	MURPHY JUNCTION	
( )	PULL	LN	60500	HOPCOAL	RED/COAL	LIZ TRK 2	MURPHY JUNCTION	

TRAIN DEPARTS ELIZABETH NORTHBOUND WITH 9 CARS (PULL-9)
END OF WORK: #44

TRAIN #290
TRAIN DEPARTS ELIZABETH NORTHBOUND WITH 0 CARS
TRAIN #290, VISIT # 2
TRAIN TERMINATES HERE
TRAIN ORIGINATES HERE, DEPARTURE: 13:09

[X]	Action	Road	Number	Type	Color	Track	Dest./(Load)	Final Dest
	DROP	GATX	68355	TANK-ACID	BLACK	LIZ TRK 1	(MT-ACID)	ACID CAR LOADING
	DROP	UTLX	61731	TANK-ACID	BLK/YEL	LIZ TRK 1	(MT-ACID)	ACID CAR LOADING
	DROP	LN	60555	HOPCOAL	RED	LIZ TRK 1	(MT-COAL)	TCC TIPPLE
	DROP	UTLX	61114	TANK-ACID	BLK/YEL	LIZ TRK 1	(MT-ACID)	ACID CAR LOADING
	DROP	GATX	68123	TANK-ACID	BLACK	LIZ TRK 1	(MT-ACID)	ACID CAR LOADING
	DROP	UTLX	61245	TANK-ACID	BLK/YEL	LIZ TRK 1	(MT-ACID)	ACID CAR LOADING
	DROP	GATX	68247	TANK-ACID	BLACK	LIZ TRK 1	(MT-ACID)	ACID CAR LOADING
	DROP	GATX	67951	TANK-ACID	BLACK	LIZ TRK 1	(MT-ACID)	ACID CAR LOADING
	DROP	ACL	90003	GONDOLA	BROWN/WO	LIZ TRK 2	(TIMBER)	TACCOA LMBR 1
	DROP	UTLX	56101	TANK OIL	BLACK	LIZ TRK 2	(OIL)	TANKS@THOMAS OIL
	DROP	ACL	90024	GONDOLA	BROWN/WO	LIZ YARD TRKS	(TIMBER)	TACCOA LMBR 1
	DROP	UTLX	10299	TANK OIL	BLACK	LIZ YARD TRKS	(OIL)	TANKS@THOMAS OIL
	DROP	UTLX	49721	TANK OIL	BLACK	LIZ YARD TRKS	(OIL)	TANKS@THOMAS OIL
	DROP	SOU	272344	BOXCAR	BROWN	LIZ YARD TRKS	(BAGFEED)	PENLAND SUPPLY
	DROP	PFE	96659	REEFERICE	ORANGE	LIZ YARD TRKS	(PEACHES)	IGA DR 1
	DROP	PFE	50147	REEFERICE	ORANGE	LIZ YARD TRKS	(PEACHES)	IGA DR 1
	DROP	PFE	95882	REEFERICE	ORANGE	LIZ YARD TRKS	(PEACHES)	IGA DR 1
	DROP	CRR	60010	COVHOPPER	GRAY	LIZ YARD TRKS	(GRAVEL)	UPPER MTN COAL&SUPPLY
	DROP	NKP	99714	COVHOPPER	BLACK	LIZ YARD TRKS	(SAND)	UPPER MTN COAL&SUPPLY
	DROP	LN	24589	FLATTIMBER	RED	LIZ YARD TRKS	(MT-FLATTIMB)	NUCKOLS WOODYARD

END OF WORK: #290
TRAIN #120

This switch list for the yard crew on the Tri-State Model Railroaders layout was generated using JMRI. The report is color coded to make it easier to read. After arrival of inbound trains on the arrival/departure track, cars are switched into yard tracks listed under the TRACK column.

31

TRAIN MANIFEST #44		PAGE - 1 -		2/2/2020 9:37

L&N TSMRI

TSMRI-L&N OLD LINE

MANIFEST FOR TRAIN #44-

SCHEDULED WORK FOR ELIZABETH

[X]	Action	Track	Road	Number	Color	Type	Dest./(Load)	Dest. Track/(Final Dest)
( )	PULL	LIZ TRK 2	CG	6001	RED	BOXCAR	TATE	(MURPHY JUNCTION)
( )	PULL	LIZ YARD TRKS	PRR	85328	RED	BOXCAR	ELLIJAY	PENLAND SUPPLY
( )	PULL	LIZ YARD TRKS	SHPX	10169	BLACK	TANK OIL	ELLIJAY	TANKS@THOMAS OIL
( )	PULL	LIZ TRK 2	CB&Q	188734	RED	GONDOLA	BLUE RIDGE	TACCOA LMBR 1
( )	PULL	LIZ TRK 2	LN	49409	BROWN	GONDOLA	BLUE RIDGE	TACCOA LMBR 1
( )	PULL	LIZ TRK 2	CB&Q	188080	BROWN	GONDOLA	BLUE RIDGE	TACCOA LMBR 1
( )	PULL	LIZ TRK 2	SAL	22209	BROWN	BOXCAR	MURPHY JUNCTION	LOWER MTN COAL&SUPPLY
( )	PULL	LIZ TRK 2	NW	49300	BROWN	BOXCAR	MURPHY JUNCTION	LOWER MTN COAL&SUPPLY
( )	PULL	LIZ TRK 2	LN	60500	RED/COAL	HOPCOAL	MURPHY JUNCTION	UPPER MTN COAL&SUPPLY

TRAIN DEPARTS ELIZABETH NORTHBOUND WITH 9 CARS (PULL-9)

SCHEDULED WORK FOR TATE

[X]	Action	Track	Road	Number	Color	Type	Dest./(Load)	Dest. Track/(Final Dest)
	DROP	GA MARBLE_BOXCAR	CG	6001	RED	BOXCAR	(MT-BOX)	

TRAIN DEPARTS TATE NORTHBOUND WITH 8 CARS (DROP-1)

SCHEDULED WORK FOR ELLIJAY

[X]	Action	Track	Road	Number	Color	Type	Dest./(Load)	Dest. Track/(Final Dest)
	DROP	PENLAND SUPPLY	PRR	85328	RED	BOXCAR	(BAGFEED)	
	DROP	TANKS@THOMAS OIL	SHPX	10169	BLACK	TANK OIL	(OIL)	

TRAIN DEPARTS ELLIJAY NORTHBOUND WITH 6 CARS (DROP-2)

SCHEDULED WORK FOR BLUE RIDGE

[X]	Action	Track	Road	Number	Color	Type	Dest./(Load)	Dest. Track/(Final Dest)
( )	PULL	TACCOA LMBR 2	CB&Q	120611	RED	BOXCAR	MURPHY JUNCTION	LOWER MTN TEAM TRACK
( )	PULL	BR HOUSE TRACK	LN	8516	BROWN	BOXCAR	COPPERHILL	(TENNESSEE COPPER CO)
( )	PULL	BR FREIGHT HOUSE	LN	90153	RED/BLK	BOXCAR	COPPERHILL	(MINERAL BLUFF)
( )	PULL	BR FREIGHT HOUSE	LN	90150	RED/BLK	BOXCAR	COPPERHILL	(MINERAL BLUFF)
	DROP	TACCOA LMBR 1	CB&Q	188734	RED	GONDOLA	(TIMBER)	
	DROP	TACCOA LMBR 1	LN	49409	BROWN	GONDOLA	(TIMBER)	
	DROP	TACCOA LMBR 1	CB&Q	188080	BROWN	GONDOLA	(TIMBER)	

TRAIN DEPARTS BLUE RIDGE NORTHBOUND WITH 7 CARS (PULL-4) (DROP-3)

SCHEDULED WORK FOR MURPHY JUNCTION

[X]	Action	Track	Road	Number	Color	Type	Dest./(Load)	Dest. Track/(Final Dest)
( )	PULL	UPPER MTN COAL&SUPP	NC&StL	47124	BROWN	HOPCOAL	COPPERHILL	(TENNESSEE COPPER CO)
	DROP	LOWER MTN COAL&SUPP	SAL	22209	BROWN	BOXCAR	(MARBLECHUNKS)	
	DROP	LOWER MTN COAL&SUPP	NW	49300	BROWN	BOXCAR	(MARBLECHUNKS)	
	DROP	LOWER MTN TEAM TRAC	CB&Q	120611	RED	BOXCAR	(DIM-LUMBER)	
	DROP	UPPER MTN COAL&SUPP	LN	60500	RED/COAL	HOPCOAL	(COAL)	

TRAIN DEPARTS MURPHY JUNCTION NORTHBOUND WITH 4 CARS (PULL-1) (DROP-4)

A switch list for a local train on the Tri-State Model Railroaders lists the switching required in each town along the line. The JMRI program automatically selects the cars to be switched and generates the switch list.

not create two switching orders at B. Multiple trains can be assigned to a given route, so that you can have, as an example, morning and afternoon trains working the same route.

The final section is the TRAINS section. Here you enter the various switch jobs, locals or express trains that you have planned for your layout.

Locals are trains that take cars from a yard or CLASSIFICATION/INTERCHANGE (C/I) to and from industries, while express trains take cars from staging or C/I yard to another C/I yard for later distribution to industries by a local train.

Click the ADD button, then enter the name of the switch job or train. Once your trains have been defined, this screen allows you to build and preview the switch lists for them.

When you are happy with the results, you can then print the necessary documents. This part of OperationsPro

is the area that generates the most questions in the Users forum, but there are also good tools to help you.

If your trains are not being built as expected, be sure to turn on the BUILD REPORTS option. This will show which cars are not being assigned and why.

While it may sound a bit complicated at first to set up and get running, there is a lot of value in having automatically generated switch lists for your layout. Another benefit is that OperationsPro will build trains with the least used freight cars that meet the industries' car requirements. This way all your rolling stock will get equal usage over time.

Phil Abernathy, member of the Tri-State Model Railroad Club, tsmri. org, has been using the JMRI switch list program for some time and it has helped enormously with organizing and running the operating sessions on the large club layout.

Phil has set up switch lists for locals and the yard crews in different formats to make them easier to read, **31**. In addition, he has reports that help with setting up the trains for each operating session. The JMRI switch list program has a lot of benefits and can be adapted to most operating scenarios.

RailQuik switch list program

Joe Atkinson developed the RailQuik program to allow him to have switch lists generated by a computer program for his model railroad. Joe explains how he developed the program and the various switch list reports it generates.

"Modeling the modern era, I spent many years in search of a computer-based car forwarding system to closely replicate the train, yard, and interchange lists used by my prototype. Also, I wanted to be able to specify the ratio of moves relative to one another based on my prototype's data in order

```
05/10/05 20:39 FAX 3192985454   IA INTERSTATE RR CST SVC -> NEWTON DEPOT 001
05/10/05  IAIS        Placement Instructions              Page 1
20:37:48                                                  RSGWPFR
--------------------------------------------------------------------
Train ID BICB09       Origin Station BLUISLA   Destination Station COUBLUF
Last Station NEWTON                            Departed 05/10/05 22:07
Conductor CASON       Engineer VOEGTLIN        Trainman
Crew on Duty 22:00  Relieved    12 Hours Up 10:00
WEST TRAIN EX NEWTON C/F 2200 05/10
--------------------------------------------------------------------
                                                H H F          EDI
Track Seq Car    LE Block To           Station KD  W Z B Commodity BOL

      IAIS   400 O     ___ ___ ___            D      ENGINE
      IAIS   718 O     ___ ___ ___            D      ENGINE
      IAIS   707 O     ___ ___ ___            D      ENGINE
--------------------------------------------------------------------
      IMRL 68721 E NSTAR DSM DESMOIN DESMOIN  E      **EMPTY**
--------------------------------------------------------------------
      IAIS  7603 E AGT IAIS ADA ADAIR ADAIR   C      **EMPTY**
      IAIS  7322 E AGT IAIS ADA ADAIR ADAIR   C      **EMPTY**
--------------------------------------------------------------------
      IATR  8364 E DISPO ATL ATLANTI ATLANTI  C      **EMPTY**
      IAIS  7497 E DISPO ATL ATLANTI ATLANTI  C      **EMPTY**
      NOKL 818914 E DISPO ATL ATLANTI ATLANTI C      **EMPTY**
      IATR  8383 E DISPO ATL ATLANTI ATLANTI  C      **EMPTY**
      IAIS  7518 E DISPO ATL ATLANTI ATLANTI  C      **EMPTY**
      AEX   8498 L PELLETT ATL ATLANTI ATLANTI C  Y  AMMONIUM N
*** HAZARDOUS ***
      RRBX  4207 E UP COB COUBLUF COUBLUF     T  Y  MG CHLORD
*** HAZARDOUS ***
      IBT  19515 E UP COB COUBLUF COUBLUF     B      **EMPTY**
      ARMN 992989 L UP COB COUBLUF COUBLUF    R      MEAT FRSH
      ARMN 765183 L UP COB COUBLUF COUBLUF    R      MEAT FRSH
      UPFE 461434 L UP COB COUBLUF COUBLUF    R      MEAT FRSH
      HLTX  7209 E BNSF COB COUBLUF COUBLUF   C      **EMPTY**
      ACFX 99675 E UP COB COUBLUF COUBLUF     C      **EMPTY**
      FPAX 820128 E UP COB COUBLUF COUBLUF    C      **EMPTY**
      HS 902528 LL RAMP COB COUBLUF COUBLUF   P      2 C/TOFC
      HS 902530 LL RAMP COB COUBLUF COUBLUF   P      2 C/TOFC
      HS 902050 LL RAMP COB COUBLUF COUBLUF   P      2 C/TOFC
      TR 526120 K UP COB COUBLUF COUBLUF      H      **EMPTY**
      MP 588014 E UP COB COUBLUF COUBLUF      H      **EMPTY**
      UP 39917 E UP COB COUBLUF COUBLUF       H      **EMPTY**
```

This report shows a train list, indicating to a train crew where any cars to be spotted to customers or set out to intermediate yards should go. From left to right, the data shown includes the car's reporting mark, whether it's loaded or empty, the customer or railroad and town/station to which it should be spotted or set out, car type indicator, and commodity. Note that, even when empty, cars marked HAZARDOUS such as RRBX 4207 still indicate the car's previous contents rather than "**EMPTY**" due to the dangerous nature of residual contents and fumes.

```
05/10/05  IAIS         Yard Report              Page 1
20:41:16                                        RSRAPFR
                       FORMAT: Switch List #1
Cars Printed East To West

TRACK: ATL1                          STATION: ATLANTIC
                                               H B H F
Seq Car    LE Switch Instr  Block To   Tons KD Z O W B Commodity

1 IAIS 7800 E              DISPO ATL   30  C          **EMPTY**
2 IATR 8321 E              DISPO ATL   31  C          **EMPTY**
LOADS  0 EMPTY  2 LOCOS  0 CARS: 2     TONS:  61  LENGTH: 114

TRACK: ATL3                          STATION: ATLANTIC
                                               H B H F
Seq Car    LE Switch Instr  Block To   Tons KD Z O W B Commodity

1 IAIS 9007                           M
LOADS  0 EMPTY  0 LOCOS  0 CARS: 0     TONS:      LENGTH: 55

TRACK: HARLAN                         STATION: ATLANTIC
                                               H B H F
Seq Car    LE Switch Instr  Block To   Tons KD Z O W B Commodity

1 NOKL 819216 L            CIC   IOW   132 C          CORN
2 NOKL 822489 L            CIC   IOW   132 C          CORN
3 NOKL 818506 L            CIC   IOW   132 C          CORN
LOADS  3 EMPTY  0 LOCOS  0 CARS: 3     TONS: 396  LENGTH: 174
```

A yard report shows the cars tied down on every track for the portion of the railroad being reported. Cars with a BLOCK TO value equivalent to their current location, such as IAIS 7800 (tied down on ATL1, with a BLOCK TO value of "DISPO ATL") are to be left on-spot, while those where the BLOCK TO and the current location differ are to be pulled.

"I made RQ available as freeware to anyone interested in trying it, but since I designed it for my own use, it requires a fair number of Access updates in order to customize it for another prototype (e.g. changing all "IAIS" references to your prototype, updating train symbols, etc.). That work may be challenging and a bit time-consuming, depending on your familiarity with Access.

"While you don't have to know Access in order to do it, you do need a desire to dig in and learn a bit about it. I had never touched it before starting this project, so if I can develop it from scratch (admittedly with the help of some Access-knowledgeable friends and online user groups), I believe the updates are well within reach of anyone who's serious about taking this on.

"With your railroad-specific updates in place and your locomotive, car, and shipment information entered in the database, the system will be ready to use.

"The first step is to generate an operating session. RQ will do so based on the car ratios you provide, meaning that car moves that happened every

```
05/11/05  IAIS         Interchange Report       Page 1
06:03:29                                        RSRAPFR

TRAIN ID BNSF 05 11 DATE 05/11/05 Time 06:03  Type ICHR
Station COUBLUF  COUNCIL BLUFFS                Road BNSF
Car        LE KD Commodity Block To   Station
CIC    2044 E C  **EMPTY*  CIC        IOW IOWACIT
BN     523067 L H VOLCANIC COUNTRY    ROC ROCISLA
IAIS   7469 E C  **EMPTY*  DISPO      ATL ATLANTI
IAIS   8070 E C  **EMPTY*  DISPO      ATL ATLANTI
IAIS   8072 E C  **EMPTY*  DISPO      ATL ATLANTI
NOKL   819218 E C **EMPTY* DISPO      ATL ATLANTI
BN     461995 E C **EMPTY* HANCOCK    HAN HANCOCK
BN     467229 E C **EMPTY* HANCOCK    HAN HANCOCK
BNSF   430669 E C **EMPTY* HANCOCK    HAN HANCOCK

TRAIN ID UP   05 11 DATE 05/11/05 Time 06:03  Type ICHR
Station COUBLUF  COUNCIL BLUFFS                Road UP
Car        LE KD Commodity Block To   Station
TTZX   857087 E F **EMPTY* AGT UP     ERR
CNW    135292 L H VOLCANIC COUNTRY    ROC ROCISLA
UP     39978 L H VOLCANIC COUNTRY     ROC ROCISLA
DRGW   12265 L H VOLCANIC COUNTRY     ROC ROCISLA
IAIS   30080 E E **EMPTY* GERDAU L    WIL WILTON
TR     526492 L E SCRAP ST ICE        DAV DAVENPO
ECUX   844299 L C PLASTIC MAYTAG      NEW NEWTON
DJJX   3749 E G **EMPTY* MAYTAG       NEW NEWTON
ARMN   765092 E R **EMPTY* MILLARD    IOW IOWACIT
UTLX   11360 L T PHOSPHOR TWINSTAT    DUR DURANT
*** HAZARDOUS ***
** END OF REPORT
```

An interchange report indicates cars that are inbound from other railroads for interchange to ours.

day on the prototype will be generated much more frequently than those that only occurred once or twice a month.

"Once op session data is generated within RQ, appropriate reports can be produced for the crews, including train lists showing where each car in a train should be set out, yard lists showing the cars on each track and whether they should be pulled or left on-spot, and interchange lists showing the cars inbound from other railroads. Following the session, RQ will update car status, moving Inbound cars to On-spot, On-spot cars to Outbound, etc., preparing all cars on the layout for their next movement.

"To download RQ, ensure you have a licensed copy of Microsoft Access installed on your PC, then visit, http://www.iaisrailfans.org/info/RailQuik , and download the appropriate .ZIP file for your version of Access. In order to update RQ for your railroad, follow the instructions at http://www.iaisrailfans.org/gallery/RailQuik-distribution.

"Sample RQ reports are shown in 32, 33, and 34. While the format of each varies from one another on the prototype due to differing purposes, the information presented is virtually identical in all. It should be noted that, regardless of report, the Block To value is the key piece of information used in determining a car's destination.

to generate an accurate mix of traffic.

"Finally, it was critical for me that the system support my prototype's practice of routing "dispo" (AKA "open disposition") empty covered hoppers to storage, then assigning them to an elevator once additional car orders are received. A tall order!

"Not finding anything available commercially that met my criteria, in 2013 I decided to develop what I wanted using Microsoft Access, completing the work about six months later. I called the resulting program "RailQuik" (RQ), as it allowed me to shorten the time it took to prepare for an operating session from several hours to around 30 minutes, and it does so through a user interface that's based on the appearance of applications used by my prototype.

Conducting operating sessions

Making your guests feel comfortable and welcome on your layout

Once you have your model railroad built and have selected how you are going to operate your layout, it's time to schedule and host an ops session. Your model railroad does not have to be "finished" to host an ops session; you can hold one as soon as you have it operational. Before you invite some friends over for an ops session, you need to prepare the layout and provide a comfortable environment for the operators. You also need to establish rules and procedures for your operators that can be discussed at a pre-operations briefing. While setting up operating sessions involves some work, it is all worth it when you see your layout come to life and your friends enjoy the ops session.

Above: The conductor ensures the crossing is clear before advising the locomotive engineer to pull ahead and cross Highway 53 in Tate, Ga., re-creating a scene similar to the photo at left. Tom permits his operators to imagine they are working on the prototype Georgia Northeastern by staying true to the prototype. The backdrop photo was taken at the same location modeled on the prototype.

Left: The crew is headed south with loads to interchange with CSX in Marietta, Ga. *Scott Chatfield*

Model railroad operations

Model railroads have often been referred to time machines, as they take us back to a time or place we have chosen to model. When we begin operating our model railroads it takes that time machine experience to the next level. Holding operating sessions lets us appreciate what it was like to work on the prototype even if we never did it professionally, **1**. Let's take a look at what is involved in hosting and conducting operating sessions.

When should you hold your first operating session? I recommend holding one as soon as you have the layout operational and can run trains. You don't need to have all the scenery installed and the structures built to host an ops session. It is actually better to hold a session before committing to scenery and structures, as nothing tests a layout like having a crowd over to run your layout. During these initial sessions you can identify issues and correct them before they become more difficult to fix once ballast and scenery are in place.

For structures you have not constructed yet, a sign placed along

the siding can indicate the industry planned for that location. It really does not impact operations to only have a sign—it just looks more realistic once you have a structure built.

Temporary cardstock structures can also be built to test how a structure will impact operations if it is going to be large and possibly interfere with access to the cars or turnouts. On my GNRR layout I used stand-in structures from my previous layout to give operators a sense of the facility that would eventually occupy the location until I had a chance to scratchbuild or kitbash a structure, **2**. As I built structures based on the prototype facilities, the temporary structures were replaced and sold at train shows.

Hosting operating sessions

Before you plan your first operating session, you need to prepare the layout. This involves not only checking the track, turnouts, and electrical system, but checking the locomotives and rolling stock as well. You should have a "trial run" to identify any potential issues. This does not have to be

done all at one time, but each train scheduled to be run should be tested. Any issues found need to be addressed and corrected before the full ops session is scheduled.

A comfortable layout environment goes a long way to having a successful operating session, **3**. Ideally, the layout room should be climate-controlled and have good lighting. If your layout is in a basement, having carpeting or rubber mats instead of a bare concrete floor reduces stress when standing for long periods of time, and greatly improves the comfort of the operators. Also, having a place for operators to sit between assignments makes longer ops sessions more enjoyable. Time and money spent to have an ergonomic and comfortable setting for your layout is rewarded when operators want to come back to operate on your layout.

Adding signs and track diagrams, **4**, to your layout help operators during an ops session. The signs can be professionally made, or designed on a computer and printed at home. If the layout is complex, signs and track diagrams can save answering lots of questions as the crew switches

2

The use of temporary structures allows for early operating sessions. Signs placed on the structures or layout help crews to identify and switch the industry, even if a finished structure is not there.

3

Wide aisles, excellent lighting and a comfortable operating environment are evident on Mike Armstrong's Rock Island Railroad layout. Mike's son, Tom, operates a mainline Rock Island freight train through Minnesota on the upper level, while his other son, Mark, is handling switching duties at Trenton, Mo., on the lower level. *Mike Armstrong*

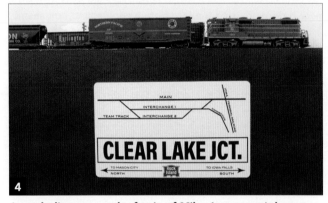

4

A track diagram on the fascia of Mike Armstrong's layout assists operators with determining the track names and spotting locations for cars. While a layout owner will be familiar with the location names, industries, and track layout, guests normally will not be. Having some helpful signs and diagrams will contribute to a smoother operating session. Mike had his fascia labels printed on vinyl material with an adhesive backing, so installation was as easy as peel and stick. *Mike Armstrong*

5

Joining a local model railroad club, such as the Tri-State Model Railroaders club pictured here, is a great way to recruit operators for your layout. At local train clubs you will find members enjoy operations and can invite them over to operate on your layout.

and operates on your layout. Having company signs on the industries also assists crews spotting cars and lets them know they are in the right locations.

Once you have the layout and the room ready, where do you find operators for your layout? One of the best places to find operators is to join an operations group or local club that holds operating sessions, **5**. There you'll find modelers who already enjoy operating and might be willing to come over to operate on your layout. Another excellent resource is the OpSIG group (opsig.org), which has a

Callboard listing of regular operating layouts and events.

Some model railroaders are hesitant to join an operating session because they feel that they won't know what to do, or will be embarrassed if they do something wrong. A layout owner's helpful and positive attitude can go a long way to making new operators feel welcomed. If it is a guest's first time operating on your layout, hold a one-on-one briefing prior to the regular crew briefing. This is a good time to show them the layout, give helpful tips, and provide information on their assigned job, **6**. This little step

helps a new operator feel comfortable and relieve some of the stress that can occur when operating for the first time on a new layout.

With a small switching layout it is easier to hold operating sessions with only a few operators and view the session as a training opportunity rather than a strictly scheduled ops session. By only operating a few trains and being able to answer questions it helps the new operator feel comfortable and enjoy the session, instead of being afraid of doing something wrong. Once they have a successful ops session, they will be more willing to come back

6

Anthony Gerard is running a locomotive in Tate Yard to become familiar with the controls and operation of the ProtoThrottle. Once the short training session was complete, he felt comfortable using the throttle and the ops session began. Giving operators a one-on-one briefing prior to an ops session is helpful for new guests to your layout. During this time, the guest can be given a tour of the layout and important aspects discussed. On Tom's layout, operators are given a chance to practice with the ProtoThrottle prior to the start of the ops session.

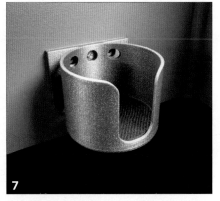

7

Providing drink holders, like this one on Scott Thornton's layout, help keep operators from placing beverages on the layout or locations where they could easily spill. Layout owners need to inform guests during the crew briefing if drinks are allowed in the layout room. *Scott Thornton*

8

A crew briefing should take place prior to any operating session. At the briefing, the host should introduce any new guests and review the rules of the model railroad. Jared Harper, left, reviews the switch list and crew instructions with Ron Long, center, and Tom Patterson for his Santa Fe Alma Branch layout.

again, learning and improving with each ops session.

One rule that the layout owner needs to establish for their ops sessions is if food and/or beverages are allowed in the layout room. There are different opinions on this subject, but in no case is it permissible to place a drink or food on the layout surface. If drinks are allowed in the layout room, drink holders need to be provided, **7**. Many layout owners provide a crew lounge where they only allow food and beverages to be consumed there. Another option is to serve food prior to or after an ops session. It is all up to the layout owner to set the rules, and guests should abide by the owners requests.

Just prior to an ops session a crew briefing should take place, **8**. This briefing replicates what the prototype crews do at the beginning of each shift, so it is very prototypical. The briefing should include any recent changes to the layout or operational issues. The layout owner should also review the paperwork used for the layout, and answer any questions if operators are

not familiar with the train authority control system or the switching documents. In addition, all guests should be introduced to the group during the briefing by the layout owner.

During the briefing, crew assignments can be given if they were not allocated before the ops session. Layout owners use various systems to assign jobs, and many rely on seniority to choose specific jobs. While seniority works well as long as everyone can make an ops session, crew members should be cross-trained to be able to fill in and learn various jobs on the layout if one of the "regulars" can't make an ops session. If possible, having a new operator "cub" with an experienced member is a great way to teach them how to operate on the layout. It gives them an opportunity to learn and reduces the stress of being on their own.

Accidents can and do happen during an ops session. The best practice is to encourage operators to report the damage to the layout owner, rather than let them discover it later. A courteous attitude by the layout owner toward operators who report damage or issues promotes a positive working environment.

The layout owner should also establish rules about allowing crew members to re-rail cars, or stipulate if the layout owner is the only one allowed to do it. Care should always

be used when reaching into a layout to perform any operation and watch for loose clothing to prevent catching it on details, **9**.

Any problems found with specific cars or locomotives should be reported on a bad order form. Having this information written down will help the layout owner with repairing the defective item days or weeks after the ops session, and not having to rely on memory.

Once the operating session is completed, it is time to perform some follow up. The layout owner should solicit feedback from operators on what worked and what could be improved. Being open to constructive criticism allows a layout owner to improve the operating sessions, and work through any issues that might not have been considered. Sending out a thank you email to all participants also encourages feedback, and creates a positive experience for all.

Two-person crews

As you set up your operating sessions, one of the decisions that needs to be made is if you are going to operate with one- or two-person crews. One-person crews are sufficient if you are operating a passenger train or a through freight that does not execute any switching maneuvers. A one-person crew can

9

Reaching in to re-rail a car requires great caution. The layout owner should establish rules as to who is allowed to touch the models or if they are the only ones permitted to do so. Guests need to be aware of loose clothing and watch their elbows when reaching into a scene.

10

Jeff Bulman, right, takes the role of conductor while his nephew, Will Tate, operates the locomotive. Having a two-person crew assigned on a local switch job allows the engineer to concentrate on operating the locomotive realistically while allowing the conductor to plan the moves.

11

Using hand signals for communication during an ops session contributes to a prototypical experience for the crew. On David Payne's O scale Central of Georgia layout, Danny Carter, right, gives a hand signal for stop to David Payne, who is operating the locomotive.

12

Operating trains at high speeds reduces the realism. While most model locomotives can operate at the prototype's top speed of 60 mph or more, operating our trains at that speed does not look very realistic, and shortens the already compressed distances and time between towns. Layout owners can establish speed limits for their layouts.

easily operate the locomotive and handle any associated paperwork on these type of jobs. Once a crew needs to perform switching maneuvers, it is best accomplished with a two-person crew.

With a two-person crew, one person takes the role of engineer and the other as the conductor, 10. Assigning one person as an engineer allows him or her to focus solely on operating the locomotive, using the proper signals, and realistically controlling the locomotive's speed. The conductor can then concentrate on accomplishing the switching required and handling the paperwork.

Two-person crews allow for newer operators to be paired up with an experienced member, and have the new operator feel comfortable, knowing there is a partner who can help them. The expression two heads are better than one is true when it comes to figuring out switching maneuvers. The two-person crew concept also promotes teamwork and camaraderie between operators.

Another benefit of operating with a two-person crew is replicating the communication that occurs between crew members on the prototype. This communication can be anything from confirming the most efficient way to conduct the switching moves to using radio or hand signals to direct the

movements. This communication helps operators "get their head into the game," and be focused on the operations.

Radio communications

As we discussed in the chapter on prototype operations, communication between crew members is critical for safe and efficient operations. The same type of communication can be incorporated into an ops session. While crew members working in close proximity to each other on a model railroad may not need a radio, those same commands given by prototype crews over the radio can be given between model train crew members

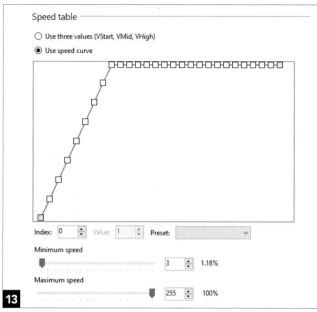

13 Programming a decoder for a "flattened" speed curve limits the top speed of a locomotive. This also allows for the operator to "notch up" with the throttle to simulate pulling a heavy load while not getting a speed increase in the upper notches.

14 Operating with a ProtoThrottle from Iowa Scaled Engineering gives you an "in cab" experience of controlling a real locomotive. The ProtoThrottle has a throttle lever with eight detents, or "notches," reverser, brake, bell button, horn lever, and lighting controls similar to an EMD control stand. The engineer must plan out his or her moves and operate slowly, which adds time to an ops session.

without a radio. The conductor is in charge of the train and directs the engineer. Distances are called out, and prototype procedures are followed when giving commands.

I have found when crews use prototype communications, the operating session slows down and moves at a more realistic pace. The crew can also talk through performing brake tests and other procedures that help make an ops session last longer.

Hand signals
While more common in the era prior to radio communication, hand signals are still used today for communications between crew members. If you are modeling the era before handheld radios, hand signals add a prototypical form of communication to an ops session. The hand signals don't have to be complicated, just the basic ones controlling movements all that are needed, **11**. The hand signals should be reviewed before an ops session just as they would do on the prototype.

Prototype verses actual speed
How fast do you want to go? Speed control is another important consideration to establish for your

model railroad, **12**. Prototype railroads establish speed limits for all tracks and yards. On our model railroads, operating trains at prototypically correct speeds may not be the best answer. Since the distances between towns on our model railroads are most likely compressed, the maximum speeds should also be compressed or reduced.

Operators need to be aware of speed limits and restrictions. Signs indicating track speed limits are required on the prototype and should be modeled on our layouts. Layout owners should perform test runs of their fleet to determine the speeds that look and work the best for their layout.

By operating at a slower speed, it adds time between points on our layouts and gives a feeling of traveling a greater distance. A note of caution is needed here too, operating too slowly can frustrate crews and cause issues. As with most things, moderation is needed with setting speed restrictions.

Speed curves
One of the many benefits of DCC decoders is being able to set speed curves. A speed curve can improve performance of the locomotive and limit the top speed. Typically, locomotives

come programmed from the factory with a top scale speed similar to the prototype. If we were to operate the model locomotive at top speed, it would soon be off our layout, and maybe onto the floor. These top speeds are generally way too fast for most layouts.

For small switching layouts, setting the top speed of the locomotive to max out at 15 to 20 scale mph is usually fast enough. Even at these speeds, it may be too fast to look realistic.

Another benefit to setting a speed curve is to replicate moving a heavy load without an increase in speed. By setting the speed to maximum about half way through the curve, it allows for the upper speed notches of the locomotives' prime mover sound to play without a speed increase, **13**. This is advantageous when starting off, or working up a grade, and makes the operation sound more realistic.

Operators on your layout need to be familiar with the speed curves and use of the throttle to simulate moving heavy loads. Some operators may not like having speed restrictions or speed curves. They feel it slows them down too much. Operating a model railroad is not a race, it is something that should be done realistically and

In this photo, Tom's son, Ryan, operates the locomotive after a brief orientation on the ProtoThrottle. The controls on the throttle are intuitive, and within a few minutes most operators are running the locomotive like a pro.

Prior to an ops session, Tom confirms the track is clean and everything operates correctly. Checking and test-running your layout a few days before an ops session is the best time to identify and correct any problems.

enjoyed. It is up to the layout owner to set the speed standards for their layout and encourage compliance.

Decoder braking features

Braking is another feature of DCC decoders that can be incorporated into your operating session. The braking function acts much like the application of the independent brake on a prototype locomotive, stopping the locomotive with greater control than just using the throttle.

To get the greatest benefit of the braking feature, the deceleration Configuration Variable (CV 04) must be set relatively high or to the maximum. With the deceleration set high, when the operator turns the throttle knob down to stop, and the locomotive coasts along until the function button that controls braking is pressed. The braking rate can be set to stop slowly or quickly depending on the value assigned. Operating a locomotive with the braking function is more challenging at first.

Since not all locomotives are programmed this way, new operators to a layout need to become familiar with the operation, and practice using the brake before an ops session.

Operating with the ProtoThrottle

In 2018, Iowa Scaled Engineering released an innovative product that

replicates a miniature Electro-Motive Division (EMD) control stand that fits in the palm of your hand. The ProtoThrottle mimics all the controls that a prototype locomotive engineer uses to operate a locomotive.

The throttle features an engine control with eight notches plus idle, a reverser, an independent brake, horn lever, bell button, and independent lighting controls for the headlights and ditch lights, **14**. Operating with the ProtoThrottle takes the experience of controlling a model locomotive to the next level of realism by placing you in the cab of a locomotive and letting you experience what it takes to operate a prototype locomotive.

The ProtoThrottle adds time to an ops session as the engineer must slow down and operate realistically, planning out his or her moves. This additional time is a real benefit to operating on a small layout as it lengthens the ops session without adding any additional track or structures. Using a ProtoThrottle takes a little training, but after a few minutes, most operators are very comfortable and thoroughly enjoy operating with it, **15**.

Ops session on the GNRR

In this final section, let's take a look at a typical operating session on my Georgia Northeastern model railroad. While my layout is not large—it can accommodate up to four operators—

I prefer to host operating sessions with two guests so the room is not overcrowded. Currently, I like to schedule operating sessions once a month by invitation or request.

Once I establish a date and a crew for the ops session, I review the switch lists and check that all cars are properly staged for the ops session. A few days before the ops session, I perform a test run of the switching moves and clean the track, **16**. During this trail run I check that all the couplers are working and there are no electrical pickup issues with the locomotive.

If I come across any issues, such as dirty wheels on the locomotive, they are fixed on the spot. I also check that I have fully charged batteries in the ProtoThrottle and the locomotive is operating properly with the throttle. Checking everything prior to an ops session prevents the embarrassment of having guests come over only to find out the DCC system is not operating, or the locomotive stalls on dirty track.

On the day of the ops session I set up the staging cassette and the removable section with the industry (if it is scheduled to be switched). I move the trains onto the staging cassette and perform a final check that all cars are properly placed for the ops session.

Normally I have guests arrive at noon and I serve them lunch. I have found that this arrangement works well as I get to talk to guests in a relaxed atmosphere before the ops session and get to know them. By eating first, it allows plenty of time for the ops session without having to worry about finishing by a certain time for them to eat. Another benefit of a small layout is that the ops sessions are more personal, as there are few operators, and everyone gets to know each other.

After lunch we head to the layout room for a brief tour and orientation of the layout if it is a first-time visit for the guests. I review the operational rules handout with the crew and answer any questions they might have. Next, I review the switch lists, instructing the crew on how to read them, and the work to be performed.

Next, I ask for volunteers to take the role of conductor and engineer. Since I have three separate switch jobs that can be performed during an ops session, I have the crew members change roles for each switch job so everyone has a chance to operate as the engineer and conductor. I have found this type of arrangement is preferred by my guests as opposed to assigning roles for the entire ops session.

Training with the ProtoThrottle is next up on the list of items covered before an ops session begins. I demonstrate how to operate with the throttle, and review the function of each control. Since most operators are not familiar with the ProtoThrottle, I have them acquire a locomotive and practice starting and stopping using the independent brake. Once they feel comfortable operating the locomotive, usually within 5 minutes, we begin the ops session.

The crew signs out on the block sheet and receives its absolute block(s) using the VBS system of authority from the dispatcher (me). The operational plan for my layout is very simple as there is normally only one train operated at a time. The crew has the authority to occupy the main and move in any direction within the block, taking whatever time necessary to complete the work.

Depending on the experience of the crew members, I assist them as necessary answering any questions and helping them formulate a plan

The end result from all your hard work and preparation is an enjoyable operating session. Stephen Floyd, left, and Paul Spilman operate the Marble Hill Turn on Tom's GNRR layout. Their smiles say it all.

to switch the industries. I prefer to let crews work the job as they see fit, rather than dictating a specific way to perform the work. Since there are no through trains or a specific schedule to follow, the operating session is very relaxed and low stress. This type of switching layout works perfectly for new operators and allows them to learn the nuances of prototypically working a local switch job.

I encourage crews to use the proper horn signals, safety procedures, and to communicate the same way a prototype crew would. This involves thinking about where a real conductor would be and what tasks they would be performing. This work includes opening gates, doors and derails at industries, and following the safety procedures outlined in the rules, **17**.

Once the crew completes the first switch job, it confirms all switches and derails have been returned to their normal positions, and then the crew signs out on the block sheet. A second and a third switch job are staged and ready to go if the crew has the time and wants to continue the ops session. Having the flexibility to hold longer

ops sessions is a real benefit for those guests who have traveled long distances to attend the session. The second and third switch jobs are operated in much the same way as the first. Some guests prefer to work the one job and call it a day. It all is up to the guest if they want to continue or not. The switch jobs are not dependent on each other and the layout can easily be restaged when the operating session is over.

After the operating session is complete, I conduct a brief review of the ops session and solicit ways to improve the session. Later in the afternoon or evening I'll restage the layout and send out a thank-you email to the operators who attended the ops session.

I hope that the review of my ops session has given you some ideas to consider for your own ops session. Each model railroad is unique and what works for me may not necessarily work for you. That is one of the best parts of the hobby, you can adapt it to suit your needs and enjoy the hobby as you desire.

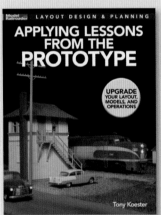
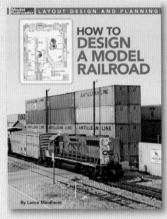

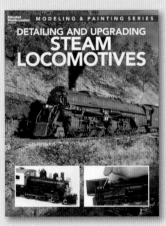